DIY Homemade Whisky, Rum, and Other Distilled Spirits

The Complete Guidebook to Making Your Own Liquor, Safely and Legally

Turn Your Hobby into a Business

By

Richard Armstrong

Copyrighted Material

Copyright © 2019 – **CSBA Publishing House**

Email:csbapublishing@gmail.com

All Rights Reserved.

No part of this publication may be reproduced, stored in a retrieval system or transmitted in any form or by any means, electronic, mechanical, photocopying, recording or otherwise without the proper written consent of the copyright holder, except brief quotations used in a review.

Published by:

CSBA Publishing House

Cover & Interior designed

By

Helen Armstrong

First Edition

2

Contents

Intro 6

Legal Matters 9

   History..9

   State Laws and Federal Regulations 12

Precautions 16

   On Blindness and Poisoning 16

   On Permits 18

   On Home Safety Tips 19

All About Safe Distillation 23

Moonshine Equipment...............................28

   Fermentation 29

   Distillation 31

      Still Choices................................31

      Be Leery of Lead 32

      Keep it Clean 35

   Heat and Temperature 38

      Heat Source Selections...........................38

Thermometer 39

Hydrometer 39

Where to Get Equipment 42

What Makes a Basic Still 44

Become Acquainted with Your Spirits 46

Of Health Benefits and Myths 47

Around the World 52

United States 52

Canada 54

Japan...55

New Zealand...55

Ireland...55

Scotland..56

Gin 57

Rum 58

Tequila...60

On Alcohol Strengths 61

Distillation Procedures 64

Corn Mash Whiskey 64

Rum 74

Vodka 85

Gin 93

Flavored Moonshine Recipes 96

Apple Pie...96

Sweet Feed Moonshine 102

Peach Moonshine 104

Lemon Cream Moonshine............................106

Key Lime Moonshine 108

Testing Your Moonshine 111

Turning Your Hobby into a Business 117

Conclusion..126

BONUS: Example Business Plan.......................128

BONUS: Liquor Laws Listed by State 144

Intro

Ah, there's nothing quite like a relaxing sip of moonshine to top off a tiring day. But what exactly is moonshine, and why is crafting moonshine at home making such a huge splash today?

Moonshine is defined as any type of alcohol that is actually made clandestinely. Usually rum or whiskey, moonshine used to be made at night (hence the term) to avoid alcoholic beverage bans and high taxes.

While the term originated from Britain, it is now used to refer to these supposed illegal whiskey stills, the production of which is conducted late at night and out of sight from the authorities.

Moonshine is usually made from sugar, water, yeast, and cornmeal, but there are plenty of variations to the basics. We'll talk about those variants in the subsequent sections of this book.

What makes moonshine quite unique is its aging— the whiskey that comes out of the still is as clear as water and is bottled that way. As opposed to commercial alcohols, which are aged in oak barrels that are charred which lends to its golden amber color. Moonshine is un-mellowed with a really, really strong kick to its taste.

While there are a myriad of guides, how-to's, and DIY tips and tricks out there on how to make moonshine at home, this book is more concerned about your safety as you're making it.

After all, you wouldn't consume something that might potentially be bad for you, right?

Because of the great dangers of making moonshine at home without proper supervision and without the proper standard checks and quality control, many home brewers fall prey to the harmful effects of unchecked alcohol.

This is why we're all about safety in this book. I'll walk you through the entire process from start to finish, including:

- How to use your tools wisely

- How to clean them thoroughly and safely

- How to maintain their sanitary purposes

- How to stay hygienic

And thorough instruction about making your precious moonshine at home, all so you can enjoy more of that deliciously sinful drink for years and years to come!

Legal Matters

Of course, above all else, it is incredibly important to first discuss the legal matters that surround this historically illicit activity.

History

For you to gain a better understanding and a deeper appreciation of everything moonshine, it's interesting to know all about its rich history throughout the years in the United States, and how the government's involvement with these legalities came to be.

After the American Revolution played out, federal taxes were placed by the government upon liquor. How exactly does the government control alcohol sales, then?

To earn back some revenue from all of the extravagant expenses of the war that drained the government's funds, there was imposed an excise tax on liquor, which, of course, did not sit well with the general populace.

These distilled spirits were made by farmers who were themselves struggling to make ends meet at the time. These farmers made a living by using corn crops and turning them into corn liquor.

The imposed tax was troublesome, and tensions between farmers and tax collectors grew to uncontrollable heights. Because of all the tension and the growing anger of the citizens, the Whiskey Rebellion took over Pittsburgh, Pennsylvania in 1794.

The secret act of moonshining then went on despite the tax. Moonshine making became even more popular particularly in the Southern states, namely,

Kentucky, Virginia, North Carolina, Tennessee, and South Carolina.

These moonshiners made their liquor without paying a single dollar for the excise tax. In order to hide the illegal tax evasion, moonshiners distilled their spirits at night (hence, the term "moonshine" was born).

Of course, these clandestine night-time activities didn't last long without conflict. Violence between fellow moonshiners and tax collectors ensued. Because of the growing unrest, the Temperance Movement was born.

The 18th Amendment to the Constitution enacted Prohibition. Now, the production or the sale of alcohol was outlawed completely.

The problem with making moonshine at home is that there are no rules to regulate the whole process. Anyone can start making moonshine from their own backyard, and if the distillation process is not done properly, the results can be fatal.

Homemade stills may be simply soldered together with no hygienic considerations, and there can be a great deal of danger when the proper equipment is not used. Lead poisoning is very much a possibility, and things may go wrong with the fermentation process as well.

State Laws and Federal Regulations

In 2010, however, Tennessee was the first to legalize moonshine, then Alabama, Kentucky, South Carolina, and Georgia followed suit. In Missouri, you can distill up to 100 gallons for personal consumption per year, only if you're 21 or older.

That said, moonshining at home is technically illegal if it's going to be used for personal consumption. But with the proper permits, you can own and operate a still if you want to process alcohol, but for fuel, which is a different technicality.

According to the TTB (https://www.ttb.gov/), the Alcohol and Tobacco Tax and Trade Bureau:

> *You cannot produce spirits for beverage purposes without paying taxes and without*

prior approval of paperwork to operate a distilled spirits plant. [See 26 U.S.C. 5601 & 5602 for some of the criminal penalties. You should also review our Home Distilling page. https://www.ttb.gov/distilled-spirits/penalties-for-illegal-distilling] There are numerous requirements that must be met that make it impractical to produce spirits for personal or beverage use.

Some of these requirements are paying excise tax, filing an extensive application, filing a bond, providing adequate equipment to measure spirits, providing suitable tanks and pipelines, providing a separate building (other than a dwelling) and maintaining detailed records, and filing reports. All of these requirements are listed in 27 CFR Part 19.

Spirits may be produced for nonbeverage purposes for fuel use only without payment of tax, but you also must file an application, receive TTB's approval, and follow requirements, such as construction, use, records and reports.

For more information about the Federal regulations regarding distilling spirits, you can read more at https://americanhomedistillers.com/ and file for a permit on the TTB website.

State distilling law is different in every state. Some states have no laws on owning a still, but prohibit the distillation of alcohol (such as Colorado, which charges a small fine if one is caught doing so) while other states prohibit possession of a still unless it's for fuel alcohol (such as North Carolina, which requires a state fuel alcohol permit).

Some states may prohibit possession of distillation equipment and distilling altogether. You'll need to Google the laws in your state to find out.

If you choose to distill alcohol, make sure to obtain all applicable fuel or spirit permits (listed above).

Additionally, check your state laws and make sure that owning and operating a still is permissible.

This is exactly why we're going to be focusing on home distilling safety in this book, and why you should always pay special attention to the way you distill your spirits (not to mention the tools and equipment you are going to be using!).

Precautions

On Blindness and Poisoning

You've pretty much heard all about it—people have gone on the record to say that drinking moonshine causes blindness and poisoning. Especially during Prohibition, reported cases of these nasty maladies spread across the nation.

So, with all of these tales, is there really any truth to these accusations?

When alcohol is made, grains or fruits that are high in pectin are fermented, producing methanol. When this methanol is ingested, it converts into formaldehyde, which, in turn, can damage the eyes severely.

In order to avoid blindness from methanol ingestion, discard the first couple of ounces that come out of the distiller.

These first few ounces contain methanol.

When it comes to poisoning, on the other hand, old distillers of the past were less careful and less concerned with safety precautions and hygienic practices while distilling. Lead contamination was rampant, as some bootleggers even used lead-filled car radiators as condensers!

Of course, the 1920s was a long time ago, and things have changed significantly over time. Modern-day whiskey stills are made properly now, using lead-free solder with all the right checks and balances to keep potential health hazards at bay.

Times have changed indeed, and those horrors are a thing of the past.

Home distillers and moonshine hobbyists follow explicit safety guidelines nowadays, making moonshine safe for human consumption.

Even though moonshining at home is technically illegal, the big brewers all had to start somewhere, don't you think? They would have practiced at home too—or they wouldn't know what they know, and they wouldn't be where they are today.

On Permits

Despite all of the safety guidelines and proper protocol, the right way to make moonshine at home is to acquire the necessary permits to begin your humble little home production.

You may opt to obtain a Federal Distilled Spirits Permit, which is what a distillery planning to sell alcohol in liquor stores should get. The problem with this is that it is extremely difficult to obtain—not to mention it's incredibly expensive, too.

Another option would be to acquire a Federal Fuel Alcohol Permit.

This is actually way easier, and the best part of it all is that it's free of charge. The catch is that you need to be making alcohol for fuel and not for personal consumption.

On Home Safety Tips

Nobody wants to go on an unexpected trip to the hospital. Keep your family and friends (and your own tummy) safe by following basic precautions with every run.

Some things are basic common sense, but it's always best to talk about these things just to make sure they're well remembered. To make certain everything is safe before you begin distilling at home, here are just some home tips and tricks you should keep in mind:

1. Don't distill inside the house.

When you're making moonshine, you must have adequate space outside in a properly vented location.

Never, never, ever distill indoors.

Distilling inside the house poses a very dangerous threat of making your house combust. It's never worth risking your life for a sip of that moonshine.

2. Always use lead-free solder.

With a pure copper moonshine still, you can safely create batches of poison-free moonshine. Resist the temptation to use old radiators, sheet metals, plastic barrels, or any other thing you find lying around the house.

Use lead-free solder as well as water-based flux.

Remember, lead poisoning is not a joke, and this kind of neglect for safety precautions is exactly why moonshining at home is mostly prohibited.

3. Do not leave your still unattended.

How long will the process of distilling take? How much time have you allotted for yourself for the whole duration?

Before you start distilling, take into consideration how long you will be running the batch.

> However long the whole thing may take, always make sure you are fully present for it.

Be sure that you have everything you need on hand and within reach so that you won't need to take your attention off the still. Running out to get more supplies is not an option!

Occasional leaks may happen, and this can be extremely dangerous if you are not around to apply flour paste and to tie a rag around it to control it. Persistent leaks are not a good sign. You might need to stop distilling and get your solder ready.

4. Be mindful of leaks.

Speaking of leakage, the fluid can drip down onto the ground and waste both your time and your money.

> These leaks can also be explosive when the vapor escapes.

Make sure to check your still properly by running some water through it to clean it out.

5. Keep a fire extinguisher within reach.

This potentially explosive substance can be a great big fire hazard, so being able to protect yourself and to extinguish it right away is a must.

> Ethyl alcohol is highly flammable.

Always make sure to keep your collection points at least about ten feet away from heat sources in the area. Locating them properly allows you to prolong the lifespan of your still—not to mention it also prolongs your own life!

All About Safe Distillation

Because we're all about safety here, you should know everything there is to know about distillation. This fascinating procedure is simply the process of boiling a particular mixture, then separating the less volatile fluid and the more volatile fluid.

> The more volatile fluid is the one with a low boiling point.

In the residue, the non-volatile particles are left and discarded. When you directly distill alcohol, you need to boil a mixture of alcohol constantly with water at 172º F.

This must contain 97.2% alcohol by volume (194.4 proof). Note that this mixture boils at 18º F lower than pure alcohol. Expecting to have more than 190 proof alcohol from your home whiskey still is impractical.

As for your heat source, be mindful of how you can keep fittings airtight.

Doing so will prevent leakage of vapors and alcohol. With an electric stove, you can easily control the heat and reduce the dire risk of letting the alcohol get in contact with open flame. Always set up your still safely to keep this grand hobby of yours fun and stress-free!

Get your fermented mash ready. A basic whiskey still requires approximately three or four consecutive distillations or runs. Doing so will help you produce a pure distillate.

If you redistill the alcohol plenty of times to 170 proof or better, you will get a purer spirit. A pure distillate is free from volatile acids, ethers, aldehydes, and fusel oils produced as by-products of fermentation. Without these impurities, your spirits will be more hangover-free.

To create a distillate with as few of these impurities as possible, run your distillations low and slow. Remember that high heat can cause your mash to just boil over. This can happen through the tubing and can cloud your distillate or clog your tubing.

Also, keep in mind that your distillate is highly flammable, so no smoking, please!

1. 170º F – 205º F

In your pot, heat your mash slowly. Gradually, the first condensate should start to drip in the receiver.

This should happen at around an hour or so as the temperature reaches 170º F – 180º F. When your mash reaches 205º F after approximately two hours, stop collecting.

Make sure to discard the residue in the pot. Throw that away, rinse it out, and then properly flush out the solid debris from your tubing.

2. 160º F – 204º F

With the distillate from the first run in your pot, heat this gradually. You can start to collect the condensate in your receiver after the temperature reaches about 160º F – 180º F.

After about an hour, the temperature should reach an estimate of 204º F. Stop collecting. By now, you should have about a gallon of 70% alcohol. Continue to throw away any residue.

3. 170º F – 184º F

Now, the distillate in your pot from the second run will heat quickly even as you gradually increase the temperature. It will rise rapidly up to about 170º F.

When the distillate drips before reaching 170º F, discard this. Also, be mindful of the distillate that trickles as it steadies into a solid stream.

After approximately 45 minutes at 184º F, stop collecting. You should now have an estimate of 0.5 gallons of 85% alcohol. Discard more residue.

4. 170º F – 180º F

With your third-run stock, turn up the heat slowly until the temperature gets to 170º F, discarding any of the ones that drip out before then. Collect it when the temperature reaches 180º F after half an hour.

By now, your distillate will contain about 90%-95% pure ethyl alcohol.

Moonshine Equipment

There is lots of equipment that you need to invest in if you want to produce your own moonshine in a safe environment. It's not enough to just pick your tools based on budget constraints.

More importantly, you need to be mindful of safety issues and proper usage instructions. We'll go through all of them, along with the precautions you need to remember for each stage of the distillation process.

Fermentation

Your fermentation vessel is one of the most important pieces of equipment that you will ever need in this risky but incredibly enjoyable hobby.

Whenever you prepare your mash, remember that you will be using both hot water and cold water, so your fermentation vessel needs to be able to withstand both temperatures. The vessel itself can be made from any material.

Be wary that not all material can tolerate high temperatures, so choose your material wisely.

Wash storage vessels are normally made from glass demijohns (carboys). A demijohn, carboy, or jimmyjohn is a container used for transporting liquids.

You can also use plastic food grade barrels, as these special kinds of plastics are manufactured to prevent warping. You can even use plastics with number 4 labels, or any regular polythene containers.

As for your airlock, just bear in mind that it should be tightly fitted to the plastic cap, lid, or cork. The airlock is normally made from plastic, and this contains a water trap that allows carbon dioxide to escape.

This carbon dioxide is produced as one of the by-products of fermentation. With the contained water and the carbon dioxide, air is kept from entering the fermentation bucket.

Keeping the air out effectively keeps the mash well protected from any kind of contamination or oxidation, which is why the airlock must be tightly secured to seal the mash completely.

Distillation

When it comes to distilling, your equipment will depend on your final product. When you want to make moonshine, brandy, whiskey, or any type of drink that's more flavorful, you can use a basic pot.

Still Choices

While the design can be pretty common, don't underestimate the effectiveness of this classic. A pot still can result in an incomplete distillation, but this actually retains the flavor of the mash more effectively.

On the other hand, if you're interested in crafting rum or vodka, you can use a reflux still. A reflux still is able to perform several distilling processes with a single run. When your distillate is redistilled many times, the result is clearer than the end product from a regular pot.

Whether you're choosing to go with the regular pot or the reflux still, these two are normally made from copper or stainless steel. A lot of distillers prefer to use copper because it can absorb aggregates like sulfur, among others.

This kind of characteristic is beneficial for the user because it reduces contamination of bacteria. It is also advantageous because of its wondrous property of transferring heat. Plus, toxic substances are inhibited. All in all, the quality of the resulting end product is greatly increased.

Be Leery of Lead

When you're using copper as the material for your still, always remember to choose one that is free of lead.

Why do you need to be wary of lead? Lead has a dangerous tendency of sticking to different parts of your body. It is extremely difficult to digest and to eliminate from your system.

Even when inhaled, your body will have a hard time trying to expel it from your respiratory organs. Over time, continued exposure to lead will damage your body severely, preventing your normal production of Adenosine Tri Phosphate (ATP). And because ATP is the basic foundation of energy that all living creatures need, your organs will fail to work properly.

When lead reaches your bloodstream, it can cause severe damage to your red blood cells. In the long run, lead poisoning causes detrimental effects to your overall wellbeing, which includes:

- Malfunctioning brain cells

- Damage to your nervous system

- Severe headaches

- Kidney damage and failure

- Behavioral changes

- Hearing troubles

- Renal problems

- Reproductive issues

- Nausea

- Stomach aches

- Seizures

- Locomotive problems

- Gastrointestinal issues

- Severe tiredness and fatigue

- Loss of consciousness

These lethal issues can be caused by acute and chronic toxicity.

> **With acute toxicity, your body is exposed to high levels of lead over a shorter amount of time, and with chronic toxicity, you are exposed to lower levels of lead but over a longer duration of time.**

With a urine test, a blood analysis, and an x-ray that checks the lining of your bones, you can see how much lead is flowing through your whole system.

Be careful of using lead-soldered stills, and always make sure that your still is clean and safe. Be wary of discoloration in your still, because copper oxidizes in reaction to oxygen.

Keep it Clean

It is therefore extremely important to clean the inside of your still before you even attempt to use it for the very first time. Clean it properly after every use after that.

> **There are many methods of cleaning your still for safety purposes, and homemade recipes can be pretty effective to keep your still safe and hygienic.**

To clean the outside of your still, you can mix one tablespoon of salt with one cup of vinegar. Add just enough flour so that the mixture will turn into a paste.

Generously apply your paste mixture on the outside of your still, and let it rest for about half an hour. Afterward, wash the surface with warm water. Repeat as needed.

Instead of using this paste, you can also use half a lemon dipped in salt to polish the copper. Wipe with a circular motion and rinse with warm water.

Another method is to smudge some ketchup onto a rag. The acidity of the ketchup can keep tarnish at bay, so it can definitely be effective despite sounding a little weird.

Rinse with warm water afterward as well. With your ketchup, you can even mix it with some lemon juice and tartar cream to scrub the copper still.

If you feel more comfortable using a chemical cleaner, you can buy Tarn-X tarnish remover from your local store. Bear in mind that this chemical does emit a foul smell.

Make sure you wear goggles, a mask, and some gloves when you are using Tarn-X to clean your still.

The inside of your still is even more important than the aesthetics of the outside.

You need to clean the inside of your still regularly to keep from transferring the flavors between batches.

If you're feeling a little lazy, you can simply rinse the still with water and leave it to dry. That step alone can already work wonders on your still hygiene.

Over time, however, repeated use wears down your copper, and you need to really clean it out to maintain the quality of your distillation.

Fill up your still with about half a gallon of water. Use a toilet cleaning brush to scrub your still.

Keep repeating with clean water as you discard the filthy batch. Let the still dry completely afterward.

Heat and Temperature

Back in the day, moonshiners used an open flame to distill alcohol, but nowadays, it's definitely safer to work with an electric heat source.

Heat Source Selections

When you are using a smaller still that has about ten gallons or less, you can use an electric stove or even a portable hot plate. You can also use a propane burner as long as you are outdoors. Don't ever use gas or an oil stove when you are indoors.

Remember, never distill indoors!

Thermometer

You also need to have a thermometer or a temperature gauge, especially when you are working on a reflux still. The thermometer helps you identify the temperature during distillation at the top of the column to help you monitor the activities that happen inside your boiler.

Hydrometer

What is a hydrometer? This nifty little gadget is basically a glass tube with graduated markings and a weighted end on one side.

It can help you measure the potential alcohol content, the sugar content, and the specific gravity (relative density) of your mixture. Depending on the density of your solution, the hydrometer will sink or float.

When it sinks, that means that your alcohol has a higher proof. Imagine it like a floating fishing bobber. The hydrometer helps to determine the specific gravity of your mixture as compared to water.

Since alcohol is thinner than water, with a specific gravity of 1.000, the float will sink deeper because of the high alcohol content. Hydrometers are also useful when you want to check if the whole fermentation process is done.

It might sound simple enough, but plenty of users interpret the hydrometer wrong because of temperature. When you measure the gravity of alcohol, it will be heavier when the temperature is too low.

On the other hand, a higher temperature results in a lighter measurement as the hydrometer sinks. This may falsely make you believe that your distillate has a higher alcohol content.

The correct way to use a hydrometer and to interpret its data is to properly factor in the temperature.

As such, your hydrometer should be able to determine the temperature that it is calibrated to.

There is a standard adjustment table that normally reads a measuring temperature of 70 °F or 20°C.

To use your hydrometer correctly, fill a jar with the liquid solution that you want to test until the liquid is approximately 2/3" from the top. Slowly insert your hydrometer. Give it a little spin to remove any air bubbles and to make sure that the hydrometer doesn't stick to the sides of your container.

Now, check the scale of your hydrometer. Where does the surface of the solution cut into it?

Make sure that you read the data properly as there may be a little raised collar of fluid that may stick to the instrument. This will linger above the surface of the liquid, so get the accurate reading by looking across the top of the solution for a proper surface level interpretation.

A true hydrometer reading will accurately tell you all about the strength of your distilled spirits, helping you control your whole fermentation process and your overall alcohol content.

Keep in mind that flavorings and additives may also alter the specific gravity of your solution.

Where to Get Equipment

A simple internet search will reveal several websites where you can buy full kits, replacement parts, ingredients, and cleaning products.

As a side note, neither the publisher of this book nor I am affiliated in any way with the websites and resources listed in this section. We do not receive any benefit from them for listing them in this book. This is purely for research and informational purposes.

One informative website that has information, recipes, and all of the equipment you'll need to get started is Mile Hi Distilling (https://milehidistilling.com).

Mile Hi Distilling also has a YouTube channel where they show you how to put together and use your new equipment. In this tutorial https://www.youtube.com/watch?v=DjZkH_RV578, they show you exactly how to set up a still from start to finish.

This process is best shown in a video rather than trying to explain the steps in print.

Here are some other informative websites for your reference:

- https://www.homebrewing.org

- https://brewhaus.com

- https://www.home-distilling.com

- http://moonshinedistiller.com/

- https://www.olympicdistillers.com

- https://www.hillbillystills.com

What Makes a Basic Still

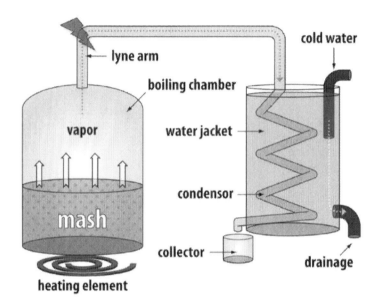

Distillation columns are made up of several components, each of which is used either to transfer heat energy or enhance material transfer.

A typical still contains several major components:

- A vertical shell where the separation of liquid components is carried out

- Column internals such as trays, plates, or packings that are used to enhance component separations

- A reboiler to provide the necessary vaporization for the distillation process

- A condenser to cool and condense the vapor leaving the top of the column

- A reflux drum to hold the condensed vapor from the top of the column so that liquid (reflux) can be recycled back to the column

The vertical shell that houses the column internals together with the condenser and reboiler constitutes a distillation column.

Become Acquainted with Your Spirits

Now that we've discussed the tools and equipment you need, here's where all the really cool stuff begins—getting to know your distilled spirits. There are so many options to choose from, and it's all based on your personal preferences, so go ahead and pick your poison.

Of Health Benefits and Myths

It's important to know that good health doesn't come from one thing alone. A proper combination of a good diet and regular exercise is key, but studies do show that spirits can help give you a nudge in the right direction.

Research has shown that red wine contains polyphenols, which are the kinds of antioxidants that you can find in grape skin. These helpful little things keep the lining of your heart's blood vessels healthy, which can also be said of resveratrol. This naturally occurring substance prevents any damage to healthy blood vessels and can keep bad cholesterol at bay.

White wine helps keep bacterial growth controlled when it comes to sore throats and tooth decay. Gin has diuretic properties. Dark beer has anti-inflammatory flavonoid antioxidants. Vodka can help lower blood pressure and reduce stress, and it can even relieve common digestive disorders.

> **Still, it's always best to drink responsibly, whatever the health benefits may suggest. Everything in moderation.**

As for whiskey, it's not only one of the world's most-loved spirits, it's also deeply steeped in common myths and hearsays.

Originating from the Scottish Gaelic term "uisge beatha," whiskey means "water of life." Now, while you don't really want to take that literally, it's still something to think about, isn't it?

Derived from a mash of some fermented grains, this particular distilled spirit is as well-known as it is commonly misspelled.

Some say dark whiskey tastes better than pale whiskey, but it is important to note that color is not really a reliable gauge to indicate the quality of an alcoholic drink.

The robustness of a drink is definitely not determined by its lightness or darkness. In fact, some whiskey brands even use no-flavor caramel in their beverages just to darken the hue a bit. These additives also help maintain the same color consistency for every batch produced, so it's definitely an unreliable indicator of quality.

Another such myth is the belief that whiskey should be consumed straight up. Truth be told, this was probably just conjured by some drunks in a pub trying to out-drink one another.

In reality, you can totally enjoy your whiskey beverage in whatever way you want it. You can go with iced, straight, with coconut water, green tea, or even with soda.

Here's a quick tip—if you really want to put ice in your whiskey drink, try to add a little bit of water instead. This will help you appreciate the whiskey even more as it opens up its aroma and reveals its full-bodied taste to you.

Now that's whiskey goodness right there!

That said, just because a whiskey brand is priced high in the market doesn't mean it's automatically of good quality. Price points are not a reliable indicator of how good a spirit is. In fact, how you define quality really depends on the drinker. It's all about your personal taste.

> While the high cost of a whiskey brand may simply indicate its rarity, your palate should never be duped by a hefty price tag.

Here's another common myth for whiskey brands: how old a drink is indicates how good it will taste.

A whiskey's age has restrictions. Just because it is aged older does not mean that it should instantly taste better. Unnecessary aging overwhelms the character of a drink, with the flavors from the wood casks affecting how the spirit should actually taste.

A drink's flavor profile depends on a variety of factors, which includes geography, grain, production techniques, manufacturing process, and the water source.

Maturation of the drink, as well as the management of the casks, affect the taste.

If you do attend wine tastings and the like, you might be able to learn more about the nuances of the flavor without allowing yourself to be swayed by the common myths out there.

Around the World

United States

Bourbon whiskey usually contains about 51% corn at a minimum. Produced in the United States, it is normally distilled at less than approximately 80% ABV, with a proof of 160 degrees.

It can be aged for two years at a minimum using charred barrels. Most whiskey drinks are aged for at least four years.

The age of the drink should be indicated on the label.

On the other hand, Tennesse whiskey normally contains 51% corn minimum. With less than 80% ABV and at a 160-degree proof, this drink can be aged for approximately two years minimum, also in new charred barrels. It can also be filtered through sugar maple charcoal.

Blended American whiskey contains 20% straight whiskey at the very least, while rye whiskey should have at a minimum of 51% rye grain. This should be distilled at less than 80% ABV with a 160 proof.

Corn whiskey, on the other hand, is a commercial product that has about 80% corn at a minimum and is aged for approximately two years minimum as well, in either new or used barrels. It is normally distilled at less than 80% ABV.

Finally, moonshine whiskey (also known as white dog, white lightning, or "corn likker") is distilled from sugar and corn mixed together and aged in either jugs or mason jars.

Bourbons can be bottled from barrels that have been specially selected from a small group and blended well together, which is called a small batch bourbon. These choices are subjective, so when one is picked from a specific cask, it is a single barrel bourbon.

Canada

Canadian whiskey is aged for about three years at the very least in used oak barrels. Most of the brands are aged for about four to six years.

While there are no strict requirements from the Canadian government regarding the percentage of grains in the mash bill, Canadian whiskey is normally made with a supplement of barley, barley malt, or rye and primarily from wheat or corn.

Whiskeys that are bottled in Canada contain older whiskeys with 86.8 degrees proof at 43.4 % ABV, while bulk Canadian whiskeys are shipped in barrels and then bottled at the country of destination. They are aged less than 4 years and have 80 degrees proof at 40% ABV.

Japan

Based on Scottish Highland Malt Whiskies, the Japanese malt whiskey is produced from barley malt that has been lightly seated and made in pot stills.

Japanese whiskeys use grain whiskey that has been produced locally, blending the beautiful combination of flavors from either Japanese or Scotch malt whiskey.

The native Japanese whiskey is called Shochu with barley, rice, or sorghum as the primary ingredient.

New Zealand

New Zealand single malt whiskey is basically malt whiskey that is distilled from a pot, while the New Zealand blended whiskey combines grain whiskeys and domestic malt in a harmonious blend.

Ireland

Based on where the alcoholic drink was distilled, the Irish whiskey is a mix of grain and malt whiskeys while the Irish malt whiskey can either be column distilled or pot distilled. It can also be a combination of column and pot stills.

> By its name itself, the Irish Pot Still Whiskey is normally a mix of column and pot distilled whiskeys.

Scotland

In Scotland, the single malt scotch whiskey is a combination of malt whiskeys from varying years. It is normally just produced at a single distillery.

Using a fire that has been stoked with dried peat for a smoky tang that adds a very distinctive taste, the barley malt is first dried over that fire for a better flavor.

When the malt whiskeys come from different distilleries, this is called a blend of "Vatted Malt Scotch Whiskey." Scotch grain whiskey contains a few bits and a small percentage of barley malt.

Blended Scotch whiskey, by its name, is a blend of malt whiskey and grain whiskey together.

As a side note, Australian whiskey is simply malt whiskey distilled from a pot.

Gin

Old Ton Gin is a sort of sweetened gin that is light and extremely popular in England in the 18th century. London Dry Gin is the more commonly dominant English style gin, while Genever or Hollands is the Dutch style of gin.

Served chilled and straight up, this spirit normally tends to have a lower proof as compared to the English gin at approximately 72 to 80 % ABV typically, and is distilled from a malted grain mash.

Plymouth Gin, on the other hand, has a more full-bodied taste as compared to the London dry gin and has a clear quality to it.

It has a hint of a slightly fruity taste and a distinct aroma that's pleasant to the palate.

Rum

White rum is light and clear, as indicated by its name. Light-bodied and subtle, white rum is filtered to remove any shade and is normally aged in oak casks.

They make really good mixers because of their subtle flavor profile. The smooth palate makes them blend well with fruit flavors.

Dark rums, on the other hand, are rich and full-bodied. They are usually produced from a pot still, then aged in oak casks for longer and more extended periods frequently.

The caramel richness of this rum is normally consumed straight up.

Now, as for amber rums or golden rums, these are medium-bodied with mellower palates compared to the darker ones.

When these rums, whether dark or white, are infused with fruity flavors, they become spiced rums.

Fruit juices are usually combined with spiced rums to make rum punches for that fun, flavorful kick.

Tequila

Rested Tequila or Reposado is either mixto (blended with sugar and water during distillation) or 100% agave. They are aged about three to nine months in wooden casks or wooden tanks with a legal period of two months, at a minimum.

The Anejo or Aged Tequila uses old bourbon barrels or wooden barrels with a minimum aging of at least a whole year. If you are looking for a really high-quality tequila drink, look for the ones that are aged for a year and a half to about three to four years.

Silver or Blanco Tequila is a clear mix that has not yet been aged. It might have spent some time in stainless steel tanks for no more than two months, but that's it.

These mixes blend well with fruit-flavored drinks and can be either 100 % agave or mixto. Finally, Gold Tequila is also unaged but has been flavored with some caramel and colored that way.

There are a whole lot more types of distilled drinks we can talk about, but that would take forever. What you need to remember is that no matter what type of distilled spirit you are into, always have fun, but drink responsibly.

On Alcohol Strengths

You can measure the strength of your alcohol by volume, by weight, or by proof. Alcohol by Volume (ABV) is usually the standard that people abide by when measuring the content of alcohol or ethanol in a particular volume of an alcoholic drink. This beverage measurement is usually indicated as a volume percent.

Remember that temperature can really influence the density of alcohol. The alcohol becomes heavier when it is cold, while it becomes lighter when it is warm. ABV then is determined by the pure ethanol's amount of milliliters in 100 milliliters of liquid. The temperature is given as 68 °F (20 °C).

Alcohol by Weight (ABW), on the other hand, is indicated by a percentage of total mass as the alcohol content in a particular distilled beverage. The formula is calculated as such:

AVB x 0.78924 = ABW x density of the alcoholic drink at 68 °F (in g/ml)

When it comes to measuring the strength of alcohol by proof, the British Parliament declared it as such in 1816, "A quantity of 100 proof liquor would have the same weight as 12/13ths of the same volume of pure water at 51° F."

In the UK, proof should be calculated as such:

100 proof = 57.06 %ABV

In the US, on the other hand, proof should be calculated as such:

Proof = 2 x %AVB

Now that we're done with the boring math stuff, it's time to dive into the delicious recipes for your distilled drinks!

Distillation Procedures

Take notes throughout this whole process. Keep practicing until you get it right. There's a learning curve to this entire operation. Just like everything else, practice makes perfect.

Corn Mash Whiskey

Now that you're fully ready to produce your batch of deliciously sinful moonshine, you have tons and tons of choices to pick from when it comes to the types of mash you can use. If you want to stay true to history, a corn whiskey mash is the best choice for you. It's a smooth and full-flavored moonshine that is absolutely irresistible.

There are many ways to make your corn mash whiskey. The "Sugar Shine" approach is popular among beginners because this method is used to create the most creatively flavored moonshine recipes out there, from chocolate moonshine to apple pie moonshine.

The corn flavored tones are normally reduced or eliminated and can result in some of the most outrageously delicious moonshine variants out there.

There is also a more toned down hybrid approach to the corn whiskey mash, where distillers augment the mash with some sugar. Economical and highly convenient, this method helps to increase the normal production of the mash with just the same amount of corn. The resulting flavor profile is also more traditional than the ones produced from the "Sugar Shine" method.

Of course, we'll walk you through the most traditional corn whiskey mash first, because basics are best.

Ingredients:

- Yeast

- Flaked corn maize (approximately 8.5 pounds)

- About 5 gallons of water

- Malted barley (1.5 pounds, crushed)

Tools:

- A long spoon

- Fermentation bucket

- Chosen heat source

- Mash pot

- Thermometer

Directions:

1. Using your mash pot, add 5 gallons of water and put your pot on your chosen heat source.

2. With this setup, heat your water to 165 °F.

3. Once you reach that particular temperature, shut off the heat source.

4. Then, add the flaked corn maize. Stir in all 8.5 pounds.

5. Keep stirring the mixture constantly for about 7 minutes or so.

Be careful when you are checking the temperature, as you want to keep an eye on that heat.

---

6. Every 5 minutes or so, stir your mixture for about 30 seconds.

7. Keep doing so until the mixture cools down to a temperature of about 152 °F. When this happens, it's time to throw in the crushed malted barley.

8. Again, keep an eye on that temperature very carefully. Every 20 minutes, stir the mixture for about half a minute. Keep doing this until the temperature drops down to about 70 °F, which should happen in approximately a few hours.

If you have an immersion cooler, you can speed up the process if you're feeling a little impatient.

---

9. Now, when the temperature has dropped accordingly, add the yeast.

10. For 5 minutes, dump the mixture between two containers, aerating it back and forth.

11. Afterward, you can now pour the mixture into the fermentation bucket. Make sure you have a good airlock and cap for this step. A spigot is also a good plus if you have it just so it's easier to pour the mixture when needed.

Fermenting your mash will require you to have your hydrometer, your siphon, and a cheesecloth within reach. Let your mash ferment for approximately a week or two at room temperature.

You should store your mash at the correct temperature because inappropriately cold temperatures can halt the fermentation process. The yeast may go dormant and waste all of your time and effort.

With your hydrometer, check your specific gravity first before and after fermentation just to see if all the sugars have been completely used. At the same time, this measurement should indicate the alcohol by volume (ABV) of your fermentation.

When you strain, you need to siphon the mash water out of the whole mixture. Make sure that all the sediments and unnecessary solid materials are left behind.

> You can use a cheesecloth to strain your mash water to make sure those pesky headache-inducing sediments are gone.

And now for the wonderful art of distilling!

You will need:

- Your chosen moonshine still

- The fermented and strained mash water

- Your column packing

- Cleaning products

Even before you transfer your mash water into your still, make sure that you cleaned your still properly from your last use. That said, you should clean your still again right before you use it, especially if you let it sit for a while since your last batch.

Make sure you pack your column properly as well with copper packing. You can either use a cheesecloth or auto-siphon to transfer your mash water into your still so that you can keep those solid materials away.

> **The goal is to reduce the sediment to as little as possible—nobody wants to have a really bad hangover, after all.**

Now it's time for the actual distillation. At this point, you aren't really creating alcohol here. You are simply separating the alcohol content from the other substances in your mash mixture. The yeast did all of the creating for you during the whole fermentation process.

Procedure:

1. Increase your temperatures slowly until you reach 150 °F.

2. Now is the time to turn on the condensing water if you do have a condenser.

3. Then, set your heat source to high.

4. Make sure that you record the time of the drips—these drips normally speed up to about 3 drips or 5 drips every second. When this happens, reduce your heat source to about medium heat.

Don't waste all that distillate goodness.

Prepare a glass container and make sure that the distillate drips here. Under absolutely no circumstances should you use a plastic drip catcher. This can lace your container with dangerous BPA. These are harmful chemicals you don't want to ingest.

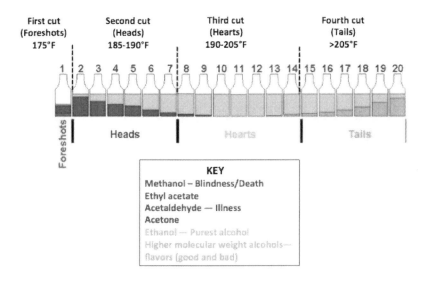

Now for a word on collecting your foreshots. Approximately the first 5% of production will make up your foreshots.

These are the earliest evaporating alcohols from your production and must be thrown out.

The next 30% are the heads which may also contain foreshots that may cause hangovers. You should throw these out too—they will have a very distinct solvent smell that's really unpleasant, about like acetone.

Foreshots contain deadly methanol.

Collect them in a separate container and never ingest them. Just throw them out for safety.

The following 30% should now be the good stuff. This portion is called the "hearts," this next part should have that smooth, sweet corn mash flavor without the harsh solvent smell.

Finally, the last 35% of the production will be the "tails," which can feel slippery on your fingers and can be a little oily on the top layer.

You can choose to set these aside, or you can just toss them out.

When you're done, don't forget to thoroughly clean your set up.

Bacteria is definitely NOT a welcome ingredient when making mouth-watering moonshine.

Rum

How do you make rum from scratch? While different locations have different methods of making rum, one thing is for certain—it's a distilled favorite for a good reason.

Production methods for rum are usually more loosely defined than vodka and whiskey, but even in its simplest form, it's still one of the most sought-after alcoholic spirits out there.

There is a wide range of flavors to choose from, and the taste differs from distiller to distiller. It all requires a great deal of attention to detail, but really, the best rum possible is the one you proudly made by yourself.

The very first distillation of rum happened on the sugarcane plantations in the early 17th century on the Caribbean Islands. Rum distillation began when the plantation workers discovered that refining sugarcane produces molasses, and by fermenting this, alcohol could be made.

As the development of the concentrated spirit of this distilled beverage spread across the American Colonies, the first rum distillery finally opened in 1664 on Staten Island. Rum became so popular that the Rhode Island rum became a trade currency at one point in time within European trading networks.

With this in mind, it's easier to remember that rum wash comes from the sugarcane plant. Produced with unsulfured molasses, rum can also be made using raw cane sugar or even sugarcane juice to gain that sweet caramel character in your rum wash.

> Because sulfured molasses has already been treated with sulfur dioxide as preservatives, it's important to use sulfured molasses. This will keep your wash from having a chemical flavor.

Ingredients:

- Molasses (approximately one gallon, blackstrap)

- Professional rum turbo yeast

- 6.5 gallons of water

- 8 Pounds of raw cane sugar

Tools:

- Long spoon

- Brew pot

- Thermometer

- Chosen heat source

Directions:

1. With your brew pot properly placed on your chosen heat source, heat the 5.5 gallons of water until it reaches 125 °F.

2. Using your long spoon, stir the raw cane sugar and molasses together. Keep stirring until the mixture is dissolved completely. This may take a while, so be patient and keep stirring.

3. You can then reduce the temperature of your mash by adding the remaining one gallon of water into the mixture. Make sure the water is cold to accelerate the heat reduction process.

4. Keep an eye on the temperature of your mixture. For every 5 minutes, stir your mixture for about half a minute. Keep doing so until the temperature drops down to 80 °F.

Again, this cooling down process can take a while and may even reach a few hours, so you can use an immersion cooler if you have one to speed up the process.

---

5. When the temperature has finally dropped down to 80 °F, it's time to add your rum turbo yeast.

6. You can then dump the mixture back and forth between containers and aerate them for about 5 minutes or so.

7. When you're done aerating, you can pour in the mash into the fermentation bucket with a cap and airlock. A spigot is a plus too if you have one.

It's important to seal your fermentation bucket with a proper airlock. Afterward, you need to store it in a dark location and maintain a temperature of about 75 °F – 80 °F.

When you ferment your wash, it's important to note that there is a difference when fermenting with molasses and raw cane sugar.

With raw cane sugar, fermentation will take approximately 3-7 days. As the yeast converts the sugar to alcohol, the wash will not have a sweet taste.

On the other hand, when you include molasses in your wash, the fermentation will take about 12 days to two weeks to complete. When the fermentation stage is complete, the sweet taste will remain because the yeast cannot convert all of the caramelized sugar.

Remember that the fermentation process is deemed complete when the air-lock no longer emits any gas.

Distilling Steps:

1. Strain the wash completely to remove any solid particles.

These solid materials can cause really bad headaches if you keep them there, so use a cheesecloth to strain your wash before you proceed to the distillation so that you can produce a more concentrated and a purer spirit.

This should also eliminate undesirable alcohols, including the blindness-causing methanol, acetaldehyde, and acetone.

2. Clean your still thoroughly, whether it's your first run ever or you've let the still sit for a while after your last run.

Cleaning your still thoroughly also helps you maintain good hygienic habits when you train yourself to clean your still all the time.

3. After cleaning, use your siphon to add your rum wash into your still, which helps reduce the unwanted sediments in your mixture.

4. Secure condensers, domes, clamps, and hoses as needed before you turn on your heat source. Increase your heat gradually, and do two separate distillation runs.

The second distillation process should separate the heads, the hearts, and the tails.

5. If you are using a condenser, turn on the water when the boiler reaches 130 °F. The still will begin to produce when the temperature reaches 168 °F.

6. Keep the distillate going as you raise the temperature gradually.

7. Using your hydrometer, check to see if the distillate measures approximately less than

20% ABV. When this happens, you can stop collecting your distillate.

8. Add some water into the distillate and dilute it by about 20%, then stir the mixture well.

9. Add it back into your still, and start the second round to enhance your final flavor.

Just like with the whiskey, the foreshots will be the first 5% of the run. Remember that this contains toxic methanol so you should throw this out.

You should discard the first 250 ml per 5 gallons as a good practice—never consume this part!

The heads will consist of the next 30% percent of the rum run. This part is also filled with toxic and volatile substances. This also includes acetone which will have a very distinct smell. Discard this part as well.

To help isolate the heads and the foreshots, keep a temperature of 168 °F for about 10 minutes. When your condenser stops producing at this temperature, then all of the heads and the foreshots have been collected.

Now comes the good part. The next 30% will be all about the hearts, so increase your temperature to an estimated 175 °F to 180 °F so that you can properly collect the good part of your distillate.

The solvent smell should now disappear, replaced by the sweet and smooth smell of ethanol.

Finally, the tails will be the last 35%. This will have a burnt type of taste or smell. You will also notice an oily film on the top of your distillate. You can discard these as well.

Aging:

The next step is the aging of your rum. The results can differ greatly all depending on your type of barrel you choose. The flavors of the rum can be affected significantly based on the amount of time that you age your rum as well.

For instance, you can expect a richer flavor and a darker result from a charred barrel, while a lighter flavor will come from a new barrel.

The final flavoring will also depend on the aging, as the longer you keep your distilled spirit in its barrel, the more time it can absorb the flavors of the barrel.

Tropical climates tend to help make rums mature at a higher rate due to evaporation, so it's a good idea to dilute your distillate before you age them, usually at about 50% dilution.

Dark rum is rum that is aged after distillation for at least 12 months.

Doing so will yield a richer rum that is darker and more flavored.

If you use a charred oak barrel and age it from about half a year to 18 months, you'll get really good results.

Using oak chips also helps give your spirit a very distinct flavor. Just remember to blend your rum well to maintain a consistent flavor before bottling it.

You can also enhance the flavor even more with some additional spices. This spiced rum can be made with peppercorns, allspice berries, nutmeg, vanilla, cinnamon, and cloves.

Don't be afraid to experiment with the different kinds of flavors and spices you can throw in. Just be sure to use separate containers if you're mixing your flavors and spices to see which one you like best.

This will make sure that you have backups in case you want to play with a few different flavors for your next batch.

For the purest, most basic rum, you can simply dilute your spirit with water and create a white rum. This lighter version should reach about 45% dilution when you blend the mix well. No aging is required.

Let the flavors sit and stabilize for about 3-4 days, or keep it in a stainless steel barrel to preserve the taste and leave the rum un-darkened.

After everything, don't forget to clean your whole setup.

Thoroughly wash everything, disassemble what you need to, and store the equipment in a cool, dry place.

Vodka

With attention to detail and a keen sense of taste and smell, you can make a really good batch of vodka when everything is planned well and executed thoroughly.

This 700-year-old art form has been steadily evolving throughout the years, especially since it was first made from distilling wine and was normally used for medicinal purposes.

Vodka used to be a low-proof beverage until creative distillers pushed the envelope and turned it into the high-proof beverage that's loved the world over today.

Skill is the key to making an excellent batch of vodka, but with practice, as with anything, you can master the craft, all while sticking to rigorous safety precautions and health regulations.

To get started, you first have to choose the best vodka mash for you. The most common variants of mash are corn, wheat, rye, beet, molasses, and potato. We'll dive right in and start with a classic potato vodka.

Ingredients:

- 25 pounds of potatoes

- 5 pounds of crushed malted barley

- 7 gallons of water

Tools:

- A long spoon

- Mash pot

- Chosen heat source

- Thermometer

Directions:

1. Use a produce brush to scrub and clean your potatoes thoroughly. Make sure you remove residual dirt from the potatoes, then cut them up into cubes. Doing so will increase the surface area.

2. In 7 gallons of water, boil your potatoes for about 20 minutes.

3. Use an immersion blender to mash the potatoes, or you can also do it by hand if you wish.

4. When you're done mashing, transfer it into the mash pot and add some water so that the total volume reaches 7 gallons.

5. Gradually increase the heat of the mash until the temperature reaches 140 °F, stirring continuously as you raise the temperature.

6. Start adding your crushed malted barley. Add 5 pounds and keep stirring.

7. Hold the temperature at 140 °F for approximately 20 minutes, making sure to stir every four minutes for 30 seconds.

8. Increase the heat to 152 °F and maintain it for an hour. Every ten minutes, stir the mixture for about 30 seconds.

At this point, try to measure the gravity. If the reading is below 1.065, add some sugar until the reading reaches 1.065.

---

9. Now, you can start to reduce the temperature until it cools down to 75 °F.

If you have the luxury of time, try to cool the mash overnight. This extra step in the process lets the barley enzymes break down the potato starches further.

Fermentation:

1. Create a yeast starter.

When it comes to your fermentation, you can create a yeast starter by first sanitizing a container like a mason jar and pouring 4 oz. of water into it. Make sure that the temperature of the water is 110 °F.

Stir in about two teaspoons of sugar, and mix the yeast in. Stir thoroughly, then let it sit for 20 minutes to allow the volume of the mixture to double.

2. Transfer the mash into the fermentation bucket using a strainer. You can aerate the mixture by making as much splash as you can, be careful not to lose the liquid as you do so.

3. Add in your yeast starter, then add the airlock. Let your mixture ferment for 14 days, keeping the temperature at room temp.

Here's a nifty trick on how you can check if your fermentation is complete. Off the top of the wash, take a liquid sample without any residual solids, and place this on a white lid or plate. Add a few drops of iodine into the sample, and check if it turns blue.

The blue color means that starches are present, which means that the fermentation is still incomplete.

Strain your mixture thoroughly to remove any solid residue that's swirling around in there. Doing so saves you from having pesky headaches and annoying hangovers after enjoying your drink. A simple cheesecloth can work wonders with straining your wash before distillation.

Distillation:

1. Prep your still properly by cleaning it inside and out. Get into the good habit of proper hygiene each time you make a fresh batch.

2. Then, add some clean copper packing in order to maximize the reflux in your column. Hook up your water input and output as well if you have a condenser. To reduce the sediment in your mix, you can use an auto-siphon for this stage.

3. It's now time to turn up the heat! Fire up your still and get started.

4. With a condenser, you can turn on your water when the temperature of the boiler is at 130 °F.

5. When the temperature reaches approximately 170 °F, your still will start producing, and you want to be sure that there is a consistent drip of around 1-3 drips every second.

As with the previous sections, the first 5% of the run will produce the foreshots, which are nasty bits that contain toxic methanol. This volatile substance has to be thrown out, so isolate them properly, discard, and do not consume.

The heads will come in the next 30% of your run. These contain volatile alcohols as well, which includes the solvent smell of acetone. This smell is pretty distinct, so you should be able to determine if it's present.

Identifying this part lets you know how to isolate it properly to steer clear of really, really bad hangovers. Just like the foreshots, make sure you throw these out.

Now comes the sweet spot—the hearts. This will be the next 30% of the run and will emit a sweeter smelling ethanol. If you have good senses as a skilled distiller, you will be able to tell how to maximize collecting this part.

Then, the final 35% of the run will contain the tails, characterized by an oily film on top of the mix. The protein and the carbohydrates here are a no-no as well, so you'll want to throw them out.

As an added option, you can also set the tails aside and run them separately in the future, if you want to get more product out of them in their own wash.

Gin

What makes gin so unique? It's the flavor of juniper berries that gets to you with every sip. The fact that it's been around since the Middle Ages only means that it's just that good.

It was initially used as herbal medicine back then, and it spread to England from Dutch and Flemish distilleries in the 17th century. Interestingly, gin was even attributed to high death rates and even the growth of the population with the social classes, leading to street riots when the state attempted to limit gin distilling and imposed stricter rules during the 18th century.

Nowadays, the two main types of gin include compound and distilled gin. Flavors for infusion are often from juniper berries, but you have complete freedom to choose any other variant that you like.

You can combine ingredients like:

- Sweet orange peel

- Cardamom seeds

- Cassia

- Cloves

- Cinnamon sticks

- Coriander seeds

- Angelica root

- Lime

- Lemon

- Anise

- Licorice powder from the root

- Rosemary

- Fennel

Once you distill your grain mash, redistill it with your mix of botanicals for you to obtain that subtle flavor and particular aroma.

The alcohol content should be around 135 proof and 150 proof if you are doing a double gin.

You can add more spices on your 3rd run, and then increase the flavor and proof on the 4th run.

The ratio should be approximately an ounce of the botanical mix for every liter of your alcohol.

Flavored Moonshine Recipes

Now that we've talked about the basics of distilling different spirits, it's all about the star of the show—moonshine.

There are tons of different flavors you can play around with, and here are just a few ideas to get you started.

Apple Pie

Is there anything more American than the iconic apple pie?

As a symbol of pride and prosperity, apple pie just happens to be one of the more popular moonshine flavors as well.

What exactly is so great about apple pie moonshine, anyway?

Apple pie moonshine can be enjoyed no matter what season of the year. It's a good pick-me-up for chillier and gloomier winter days when you need a piping hot beverage to warm up; it can keep you nice and toasty when it gets too cold.

In the summer months, you can escape from the heat of the sweltering summer sun with a glass of apple pie moonshine over ice. The possibilities are endless, or rather, the excuses to drink this delicious spirit are endless!

There are two types of apple pie moonshine recipes, and we'll go through the different prep times and methods for your mouth-watering and show-stopping flavored firewater.

The first method is quicker because you will be using a heating element to facilitate the process of bringing out the spices and igniting these flavors into your apple concentrate. This method is speedier, but there is also a greater risk of you ending up with more bitter-tasting results, so be patient.

Moonshine is extremely flammable.

You should never add your moonshine to your batch while it's simmering and on a heat source.

Another reason not to do this is because you might create a lower proof and end up with a more bitter-tasting moonshine if you do so.

Keep in mind that alcohol starts to evaporate at about 174 degrees, so adding your moonshine into the boiling apple concentrate makes everything taste horribly bitter.

Ingredients:

- 1 whole apple

- Vanilla bean

- Apple pie spice

- 8 cups of moonshine with approximately 120 proof

- OR you can use vodka with 80 proof for less potency

- Dried ginger

- 5 cans of apple juice concentrate

- 10 cinnamon sticks

- 3-4 cups of brown sugar

Directions:

1. In a large pot, add all 5 cans of the apple juice concentrate.

2. Depending on your sweet tooth, add the brown sugar-based on your sweetness preference.

3. Cut the whole apple into 4 slices and throw them into the mix.

4. Add the 10 cinnamon sticks.

5. At this point, you can create a more complicated flavor profile by mixing in about a pinch of apple pie spice, the seeds from 1 or 2 vanilla beans, and a quarter cup of dried ginger. Even just a tiny hint of these touches can go a long way when creating more complex profiles.

6. Let your mixture heat to a low simmer, then cover your pot. Let this mixture simmer for about an hour in low heat, covered.

7. Remove your pot from the heat source and let the mixture cool down for a bit. Afterward, throw in 8 cups of moonshine, and stir completely.

Make sure that your apple concentrate batch has completely cooled before you add the moonshine.

Once properly stirred, pour the moonshine mixture into quart jars, making sure to use a cheesecloth to help filter all of the debris.

You can add another cinnamon stick or about a quarter of an apple in each jar. You can enjoy your moonshine as is, but if you want a more aged flavor, seal and store your quart jars in the fridge for about 2-3 weeks, stir well before serving.

This next method is the slower one, as you will be letting your batch sit for a whole day. The next day, take the batch out of the refrigerator and mix the moonshine in completely with your apple concentrate mixture.

Because of this extra 24 hours of prep time, you will be allowing the cinnamon, apples, and other spices to really blend well with the apple concentrate for a deeper, richer, more complex flavor profile.

Sweet Feed Moonshine

There are many different types of molasses and several grains of sweet feed you can try out to make a great tasting moonshine.

There are tons of ways you can have fun and experiment with your different recipes, because why should you stop at plain moonshine? After all, you already have all of the equipment, and you can make new batches any time you want to, especially if you end up with a particularly bad-tasting batch.

Sweet feed moonshine is one of the more creative recipes you can play around with.

Ingredients:

- 6.5 gallons of water

- An 8-gallon fermenter with a lid and airlock

- Your choice of sweet feed

- 6 pounds of sugar

- A package of Whisky yeast

Directions:

1. Cover the bottom of your 8-gallon fermenter bucket with enough feed. This should be about 5 inches deep or so.

2. Add the 6 pounds of sugar and fill the fermenter with boiling water halfway.

3. Mix well until you are sure that the sugar has dissolved completely. Then, throw in the rest and finish filling the fermenter with warm water.

4. Keep filling with water until you reach 6.5 gallons of the mash. This will leave approximately 3 inches of head space inside your fermenter.

5. After the mixture has cooled down to about 75F to 80F, add in your yeast. Then, cover with your lid and use the airlock.

6. Keep this for about 5-6 days, and it will be ready to distill! Run it at approximately 150-160 proof.

Make sure to filter your mash properly and remove any solid particles and sediments as these tend to stick to the bottom and may burn.

If you want to, you can age it in oak for a few months to bring out all of the richness and character.

Peach Moonshine

Simple, user-friendly, and delectable to the palate, peach moonshine is, of course, all about the peaches.

This recipe is extremely easy to make, and it'll be great if you can buy some peaches from your local farmers market. It's always a good idea to support local farmers.

Ingredients:

- 6 gallons of water

- 20 lbs. of peaches, with the pits removed

- 2 packets of champagne yeast (about 10 grams)

- OR you can also use a packet of Pot Still Turbo with pectic enzyme

- 6 lbs. of granulated sugar (if you can, use cane sugar or raw sugar)

Directions:

1. In a 10-gallon stockpot, mash up your peaches. Make sure that you remove the pits completely.

2. Add the 6 gallons of water, and then place this over your heat source. Keep the heat up until you reach 150F.

3. At this point, add in your sugar and keep stirring. Doing so makes sure that the solid particles don't stick to the bottom and burn.

4. Once the sugar is dissolved completely, you can turn off the heat and allow the mixture to cool to approximately 80F.

5. Then, place it in the fermenter and add in your yeast. Use your airlock and ferment the mixture for 5 days.

6. Your ABV should be approximately 12%-15%. Strain your mixture and distill using a pot still.

Remember to keep about a quart of your sugar peach mixture in the refrigerator so that you still have some leftover to flavor your mixture after distillation. You can also add in some cinnamon sticks and mix it up.

Serve and have fun!

Lemon Cream Moonshine

Coffee creamer and moonshine? Yes, they do mix!

Here's a great idea to make lemon cream moonshine that you can easily adjust based on your preferred creaminess and sweetness.

Ingredients:

- Fresh lemon and lemon juice

- Sugar

- Moonshine spirit with a neutral taste

- Powdered coffee creamer

Directions:

1. In a pot, pour in 1.5 cups of water along with a cup of sugar and place this on a stove.

2. Bring it to a boil, remembering to stir continuously to make sure that the sugar dissolves well in the water.

3. Add about 2 tablespoons of coffee creamer and 4 tablespoons of lemon juice into the mix.

4. Take the fresh lemon and squeeze half of it into the mixture as well. Let this simmer for about 3 minutes, then let it cool down to room temp.

5. Once the mixture is cool, pour the contents into a mason jar or whatever container you have, and top it off with 140 proof moonshine. You should end up with about 80 proof.

6. Then, remove the pulp from your lemon, twist the rind and leave it in the jar, placing it in the freezer. Make sure to shake before drinking.

Key Lime Moonshine

Here's another zesty twist to your average moonshine that's perfect for sweltering summer days in the sun.

Ingredients:

- Coconut extract

- Key lime juice

- Sugar

- Moonshine spirit (neutral spirit)

- Vanilla

Directions:

Pour 1.5 cups of water into a pot and place it on a stove.

Add in a cup of sugar. Bring the water and sugar to a boil. Keep stirring well to make sure that the sugar is properly dissolved.

Mix in a quarter teaspoon of vanilla extract, 3 tablespoons of key lime juice or lime juice, and about half a teaspoon of coconut extract.

Let this mixture simmer for approximately 3 minutes before allowing it to cool down to room temp.

Pour your mixture into mason jars and top off with your neutral moonshine spirit.

Serve chilled.

No matter what kind of moonshine recipe you're making, always make sure you keep fire safety in mind first and foremost.

Nothing ruins a good drink faster than a nasty burn—or worse, starting a fire inside your home!

Testing Your Moonshine

Because this guide is all about safety, we want to make sure that your final product is safe for drinking, and, at the same time, incredibly delicious.

A properly prepared moonshine is all dependent on how you pay attention to it, so here are just a few quick tips on making sure everything is safe.

1. Use a pure copper moonshine still. This traditional method has its own advantages apart from being a classic. A pure copper still can absorb syntheses with sulfur, which helps reduce any bacterial contamination. A pure copper still also increases the overall quality of your final product because of its effective heat transfer properties.

When you are using solder, use one that does not contain any lead.

Lead is extremely harmful to the body and can be very difficult to eliminate. Instead, use silver solder.

2. Always use glass when it comes to your collection pot. Do not use plastic, and make sure that you keep this collection pot away from any sources of heat.

3. Make sure that you use only the freshest and most natural ingredients for your product. High-quality yeast, water, and sugar go a long way in enhancing taste.

4. Dispose of the first few bits that come out so that you can avoid the contamination from methanol.

Methanol has a lower boiling point than ethanol and is very toxic.

---

5. Ensure that your moonshine still is sealed tightly.

6. Always clean your still thoroughly before and after usage. Doing so not only helps get you into the practice of maintaining good hygiene,

but it also provides you with a good method on how to check if your still has any leaks. Leakage is never a good thing, as it lets your precious alcohol vapor escape!

If you notice a leak in your still, try to use flour paste to seal it.

If it does not work, do not attempt to continue until you properly fix the leak.

As for your barrels or your boxes, make sure that they are thoroughly cleaned as well. Smoke out your barrels and boxes after each use by setting a few handfuls of cornmeal bran on fire. Always be safe and never complete this step indoors.

7. Check if your moonshine is of good quality. If there is an unusual chemical odor, do not drink it. Put some of your moonshine on a spoon and light it on fire.

If the moonshine is red, this means that it contains lead. DO NOT DRINK IT!

If the moonshine is yellow, you risk blindness. DO NOT DRINK IT!

If the moonshine is blue, then the moonshine is safe.

But if it does not burn at all, DO NOT DRINK IT!

Always do the spoon test no matter what happens, and regardless of how your product smells. It's always better to be safe than poisoned.

8. In the case of using wood fuel, use ash wood as it gives you a nice and steady heat and smoke. Hickory and mountain oak are also good alternatives.

9. When you are running your whiskey, make sure that you keep it cold while it is running, and don't ever let it run too quickly. Doing so will help keep it mild and smooth and less harsh to the taste.

10. Sometimes, whiskey gets burned because of poor management, and the fact that it is not carefully watched over during the process.

11. Always make sure to stir while you are heating, and don't keep the fire too hot. These little details may seem insignificant at first, but your meticulous attention to detail is what will distinguish your drinks from the rest of the moonshiners out there.

There's nothing more delicious than moonshine made with love.

Be wary of these common distilling mistakes moonshining amateurs often make:

- Not testing your homemade set up well enough, especially since you are working with gas and other highly flammable materials.

- Leaving your distiller unattended even for just a second or two, therefore opening yourself up to horrible accidents due to neglect and lack of vigilance.

- Forgetting to close your tap and making a huge mess.

lislabelling your containers, or not labeling them at all. It's best to use color-coded bottles and jars if you can, especially with your ingredients. You wouldn't want to mix the wrong stuff.

- Forgetting to cover up your still outdoors and leaving it open for contamination or making it a very attractive nesting hub for wasps and hornets.

- Rushing the whole procedure. Patience is a virtue!

Turning Your Hobby into a Business

So you have the drive and desire to create delicious craft spirits. You have practiced and perfected your methods and procedures. You keep everything safe, clean, and have successfully made several batches of hooch that turned out GREAT!

How cool would it be to sell your creations and make a buck or two? I'll tell you, it's not easy. It's a long road from mash to profit. There are many, many, many hoops to jump through before you can accept any money in exchange for your yummy spirits.

How to start a craft distillery in 7 (not so easy) steps:

1. Write a REALISTIC business plan. Many online sites offer business plan creation services. You can also hire someone to help you with this.

y https://www.bplans.com or hiring someone rom https://www.fiverr.com. Additionally, local business incubators, the chamber of commerce, and community business groups offer advice and classes in regards to creating a solid business plan.

Before you create a business plan, make sure that some decisions are in order. For example, you'll need to figure out exactly what your product is, what sort of legal structure your business will take, who owns your business, where you will conduct business, and what your financials will look like.

You will need to conduct marketing research, legalities investigations (like zoning laws, legal permits, what sort of licenses you'll need to obtain), and create a budget with prospective income, expenses, and prospectus. You will need to know and taper your business plan to acquiring a business loan if you think you should pursue that route.

A business plan is your road map to success a_ it paves the way for you to stick to a process, to make firm decisions, and to examine this business realistically. The business plan should be comprehensive, but not too wordy and not too long.

You should tell your story, but keep it short and sweet.

A business plan usually contains sections such as:

Executive summary- The quick and dirty introduction to your newly formed company or business idea.

Company Overview – What is your vision? What is your mission? What are you hoping to accomplish and how?

Business environment- Discuss your business structure. What job positions will you need? What are their roles?

Company description

mpany strategy – Conduct a SWOT analysis, escribe your clientele and prospective customers.

Financial review – Be honest and be realistic. You will probably not make a million dollars in your very first year!

Action plan – Include a description of your marketing strategy. How will you do what you want to do?

You can also include any other documents and supporting information that you deem fit.

2. Start researching the art of distilling. You have already done that! Hopefully, you have a fervent desire to distill your own spirits already. Perfect your techniques. Decide on your packaging. Will your bottle/jar design be unique? What will set you apart?

3. Visit many distilleries in different states. Sounds like an amazing road trip! Call ahead and schedule tours and interview other distillery owners. Learn about this craft first

hand from those who have been there and done that. Most people will be willing to share their knowledge with you if you ask nicely.

You can read all of the books and do numerous internet searches to read all of the blogs, but if you don't see it in person, you really won't get a sense for what this business is all about.

4. You cannot have a federally licensed distillery inside your house or in some areas, not even on your own private property if it not zoned to do so. You have to select a place that you can legally set up and is zoned appropriately. This starts at the local (city and county) level, then the state level, then the federal level.

You have to be sure that your location meets all of the required statutes. You will also have to consider how you're going to run the business from that location. Will you have a gift shop? Can you (legally) have a tasting room at this location? Will you only manufacture your liquor at this location and send it to a distributor for sale? All of these considerations come into play when selecting a distillation plant site.

5. Set up the equipment completely. You have to have your equipment set up before applying to the TTB for a permit. We talked about the role of the TTB and permits in the introductory chapter of this book. Invest in quality equipment. Consider the volume of spirits that you will want to produce. Your equipment, storage space, and how much time you can devote to the crafting of the spirits all play a part.

6. Apply for federal and state permits, as applicable. To create moonshine or any distilled spirits for human consumption, you must purchase a federal license. This process may take as long as a year to complete. You must also check with your state to be sure that you are in accordance with your local laws as well.

7. Once you have your licenses, permits, location, and plan in place, put it into action! Craft some

spirits and start selling. Put your plan into action. How are you going to get your liquor into the hands of customers?

You will also have to enact some sound marketing. Hopefully, as you were contemplating your business plan, you conducted some market and marketing research. You should know about your local area that you're trying to sell to – who lives there, what they are interested in, what they think about their liquor.

You should also invest in a website that exhibits your personal, unique brand. Don't neglect social media! It's not only free marketing to have a Twitter, Facebook page, and Instagram account, it's also sound modern business practices.

Expenses that you can expect for your distillery start-up include:

- Lease/rent

- Insurance

- Utilities

- Payroll, if you have employees

- Raw material costs for items such as grain, molasses/sugar, yeast/nutrients, and packaging

- Marketing which includes everything from signage, ads in travel brochures, business cards, and more

- Excise taxes for any product that you sell

- Items to stock your gift shop, if you choose to have one

These expenses vary greatly depending on how you choose to run your craft distillery.

In conclusion, research is your best friend, especially when you're entering such a well-regulated and expensive industry like this. Ask questions. Read everything you can get your hands on. Surround yourself with the right advisors. Enlist (and pay for) help as needed.

If you choose to take this hobby of making "bathtub gin" into a profitable business, I wish you the best of luck.

In the meantime, put your feet up and enjoy a nice, smooth draw of moonshine.

Conclusion

Now that you are a moonshining master, there's nothing more relaxing than clinking glasses with the ones who matter to you the most after a long, hard day, or simply sharing a hearty chug with your best buds while celebrating your life's milestones together.

The best part of it all is that the drinks are all your proud creations, so the satisfaction of a job well done is even greater—not to mention you can customize your spirits to suit your every mood.

Just remember to be safe all the time, before, during, and after your runs. A little precaution always goes a long way.

If you stick to the safety tips and helpful warnings in this guide, you'll be distilling your fave spirits for a long, long time—and hopefully stay out of trouble with the law, too.

Happy distilling, and may your moonshine be as strong as your health!

Thank you so much for buying my book. This was certainly a labor of love.

Would you please consider leaving a review on whatever site you purchased this book? I would sincerely appreciate it.

I take all comments and reviews to heart and will try to take your opinions into consideration when I write more books in the future.

BONUS: Example Business Plan

Distillery Business Plan – Executive Summary

We R Spirited Distillery, LLC is a standard distillery plant that will be located in an industrial area Mobile, Alabama. We have been able to secure a long term lease for a facility in a strategic location with an option of a long term renewal on agreed terms and conditions that is favorable to us. The facility has government approval for the kind of business we want to run, and it is easily accessible, and we are deliberate about that to facilitate easy movement of raw materials and finished products.

We are in the distillery business to produce finely distilled alcoholic drinks such as Whisky, Gin, and Rum that can compete with any other distillery depot in the United States of America and in any part of the world. We are also in business to make profits at the same to give our customers value for their money; we want to give people and businesses who patronize our distilled alcoholic drinks the opportunity to be part of the success story of We R Spirited Distillery, LLC.

Much more than producing finely distilled alcoholic drinks, our customer care is going to be second to none. We know that our customers are the reason why we are in business which is why we will go the extra mile to get them satisfied when they visit purchase any of our distilled alcoholic drinks and also to become our loyal customers and ambassadors.

We R Spirited Distillery, LLC is a family business that will be owned by Susan B. Tonyson. Ms. Tonyson, who is the Chief Executive Officer of the Company, holds a Master's Degree in Business Management (MBA). She has well over 15 years of experience working in a related industry as a senior manager before starting We R Spirited Distillery, LLC. She will be working with a team of professionals to build the business and grow it successfully.

Our Product

We R Spirited Distillery, LLC is going to operate a standard and licensed distillery whose products will not only be sold in the United States and Canada but also in other parts of the world. We are in the distillery business to make profits and also to give our customers value for their money.

Our Vision Statement

Our vision is to establish standard distillery plant whose products will be not only be sold in the United States of America and Canada but also in other parts of the world.

Our Mission Statement

Our mission is to establish a standard distillery plant that will produce a wide range of spirits and whiskey for both low-income earners and for luxury consumption. We want to build a distillery business that will be listed amongst the top 10 distilleries in the United States of America and Canada

Our Business Structure

We have decided to hire qualified and competent people to occupy the following positions:

- Chief Executive Officer (Owner)

- Plant Manager

- Human Resources and Admin Manager

- Warehouse Manager

- Merchandise Manager

- Sales and Marketing Manager

- Information Technologist

- Accountants / Cashiers

- Cleaners

Distillery Business Plan – SWOT Analysis

We R Spirited Distillery, LLC employed the services of an expert HR and Business Analyst with bias in start-up business to help us conduct a thorough SWOT analysis and to help us create a business model that will help us achieve our business goals and objectives.

This is the summary of the SWOT analysis that was conducted for We R Spirited Distillery, LLC;

Strength:

Part of what is going to count as positives for We R Spirited Distillery, LLC is the vast experience of our management team, we have people on board who are highly experienced and understand how to grow a business from scratch to becoming a national phenomenon.

Weakness:

A major weakness that may count against us is the fact that we are a new distillery plant, and we don't have the financial capacity to engage in the kind of publicity that we intend to.

Opportunities:

The opportunities for mega distilleries with a wide range of distilled products are enormous. This is due to the fact that the average American and Canadian consume distilled products.

We know that it is going to require hard work, and we are determined to achieve it.

Threat:

We are quite aware that just like any other business, one of the major threats that we are likely going to face is an economic downturn and unfavorable government policies. It is a fact that economic downturn affects purchasing power. Another threat that may likely confront us is the arrival of a new distillery plant in same location where ours is located.

Distillery Business Plan – MARKET ANALYSIS

Market Trends

In recent time, flavored distilled alcoholic drinks (Spirit and Whiskey et al.) have become increasingly popular, especially among upwardly mobile and trendy young people. This is the major reason why many distillers have each launched their own innovative twists on their classic brands. For instance, Campari recently introduced an American Honey offshoot of its Wild Turkey brand. So also Jack Daniel's produced a new seasonal blend of apple cider liqueur, spices and Jack Daniel's Old No. 7 Tennessee Whiskey.

Another trend in the distillery industry is that most distillers now produce expensive distilled drinks for high-end clients and also normal distilled drinks for everyday people. Statistics has it that consumers have experienced appreciable increasing disposable income since 2009, and as a result, many have sought out expensive distilled alcoholic brands that are perceived to be classy and of higher quality.

Our Target Market

Our target market cannot be restricted to just one group of people, but all those adults over the age of 21 who drink alcohol and those who would want to try out spirits.

Distillery Business Plan – SALES AND MARKETING STRATEGY

Sources of Income/Sales Forecast

We R Spirited Distillery, LLC is established to maximize profits in the distillery industry in both the United States of America and Canada.

It is important to state that our sales forecast is based on the data gathered during our feasibility studies, market survey, and also some of the assumptions readily available on the field. Below are the sales projections that we were able to come up with for the first three years of operations;

First Year-: $250,000

Second Year-: $750,000

Third Year-: $1,500,000

This projection is done based on what is obtainable in the industry and with the assumption that there won't be any major economic meltdown and the arrival of a competitor in the same location as ours within the period stated above. Please note that the above projection might be lower and at the same time it might be higher.

Distillery Business Plan – Marketing Strategy and Sales Strategy

Before choosing a location for We R Spirited Distillery, LLC and also the kind of distilled drinks to produce, we conducted a thorough market survey and feasibility study for us to be able to penetrate the available market of those who consume distilled drinks.

We hired experts who have a good understanding of the distillery industry to help us develop marketing strategies that will help us achieve our business goal of winning a larger percentage of the available market in the United States of America and Canada.

In summary, We R Spirited Distillery, LLC will adopt the following sales and marketing approach to selling our distilled alcoholic drinks:

- Introduce our distilled alcoholic drinks brand by sending introductory letters to residence, alcohol merchants and other stakeholders both in the United States of America and Canada

- Open our distillery plant with a party to capture the attention of residents who are our first targets

- Engage in a roadshow in targeted communities from time to time to sell our products

- Advertise our products in community-based newspapers, local TV and radio stations

- List our business and products on yellow pages ads (local directories)

- Leverage on the internet to promote our distilled alcoholic brands

- Engage in direct marketing and sales

- Encourage the use of Word of mouth marketing (referrals)

Distillery Business Plan – Publicity and Advertising Strategy

Even though our distillery plant is a standard one with a wide range of products that can favorably compete with other leading brands, we will still intensify publicity for all our products and brand. We are going to explore all available means to promote We R Spirited Distillery, LLC.

Here are the platforms we intend leveraging on to promote and advertise We R Spirited Distillery, LLC:

- Place adverts on both print (community-based newspapers and magazines) and electronic media platforms

- Sponsor relevant community programs

- Leverage on the internet and social media platforms like; Instagram, Facebook, Twitter, et al. to promote our brand

- Install our Bill Boards on strategic locations all around major cities in the United States of America and Canada

- Engage in roadshows from time to time in targeted communities

- Distribute our fliers and handbills in target areas

- Position our Flexi Banners at strategic positions in the location where we intend getting customers to start patronizing our products.

- Ensure that all our staff members wear our customized clothes, and all our official cars and distribution vans are customized and well branded.

Distillery Business Plan – Start – Up Expenditure (Budget)

This is the key areas where we will spend our start-up capital:

- The Total Fee for Registering the Business in Alabama – $750.

- Legal expenses for obtaining licenses and permits as well as the accounting services (software, P.O.S machines, and other software) – $1,300.

- Marketing promotion expenses for the grand opening of We R Spirited Distillery, LLC in the amount of $3,500 and as well as flyer printing (2,000 flyers at $0.04 per copy) for the total amount of – $3,580.

- Cost for hiring Business Consultant – $2,500.

- Insurance (general liability, workers' compensation, and property-casualty) coverage at a total premium – $2,400.

- Cost for payment of rent for 12 months at $1.76 per square feet in the total amount of $105,600.

- Cost for the construction of a standard distillery – $100,000.

- Other start-up expenses including stationery ($500) and phone and utility deposits ($2,500).

- Operational cost for the first 3 months (salaries of employees, payments of bills et al.) – $100,000

- The cost for Start-up inventory (raw materials and packaging materials et al.) – $80,000

- Storage hardware (bins, rack, shelves, food case) – $3,720

- The cost for counter area equipment (countertop, sink, ice machine, etc.) – $9,500

- Cost for distillery equipment – $100,000

- Cost for store equipment (cash register, security, ventilation, signage) – $13,750

- Cost of purchase of distribution vans – $100,000

- The cost for the purchase of furniture and gadgets (Computers, Printers, Telephone, TVs, Sound System, tables and chairs et al.) – $4,000.

- The cost of Launching a Website – $600

- The cost of our opening party – $10,000

- Miscellaneous – $10,000

We would need an estimate of $1.2M to successfully set up our distillery plant in Mobile, Alabama. Please note that this amount includes the salaries of all the staff for the first 3 months of operation.

We have been able to generate about $500,000 (Personal savings $400,000 and soft loan from family members $100,000), and we are at the final stages of obtaining a loan facility of $700,000 from our bank. All the papers and document have been signed and submitted, the loan has been approved, and any moment from now our account will be credited with the amount.

Distillery Business Plan – Sustainability and Expansion Strategy

The future of a business lies in the numbers of loyal customers that they have the capacity and competence of the employees, their investment strategy, and the business structure.

We R Spirited Distillery, LLC will ensure that all the factors listed above are reinforced regularly, we will continue to improvise with our products and also we will engage in continuous capacity building of our workforce.

BONUS: Liquor Laws Listed by State

Alabama	State retains a monopoly over wholesaling of distilled spirits only. Distilled spirits (liquor) are purchasable in either state-owned retail liquor stores, known as ABC Stores, or privately owned retail liquor stores. Privately owned retail liquor stores tend to be open on Sundays, public (federal & state) holidays, and later hours than state-owned liquor stores. State-owned liquor stores are closed on Sundays and public holidays. If a state-owned liquor store is located in an unincorporated area, only the state sales tax and county sales tax is collected.
Arizona	Sales of any type of alcohol are legal at any store that has an off-premises

liquor license, including but not limited to convenience stores and grocery stores. Bars may sell closed containers of alcohol for consumption off the premises. Drive-through liquor stores are allowed. Everclear Grain Alcohol Proof 190 (95% alcohol) is legal. A large percentage of the land area of Arizona is in Indian reservations, many of which have liquor laws considerably more restrictive than state law, up to and including total prohibition. "Beer busts" (all the beer/liquor one can drink for a set price) in bars are illegal. Persons 18 years of age or older may work in bars and liquor stores serving and selling alcohol. Patrons may not purchase for on-premises consumption more than 50 ounces of beer, 1 liter of wine or 4 ounces of distilled spirits at one time. DUI penalties are some of the most severe in the nation. A person convicted of a DUI (even first offense) must have an interlock installed in his car for one year. Arizona has an

	'Impaired to the Slightest Degree' law that can convict a person even if his BAC is less than .08%.
Arkansas	Has numerous dry counties and other dry areas, but private clubs can serve even in dry areas. No sales on Christmas Day. Alcohol sales are permitted 24 hours a day 7 days a week regardless of holiday in-state casinos.
California	Relatively unrestricted; beer, wine, and liquor available at grocery stores, convenience stores, gas stations, and warehouse clubs. No statewide holiday restrictions. Motor vehicles entering from Mexico may only import 1 liter of alcohol (duty-free). Sale or distribution of grain alcohol higher than 60% ABV is illegal, but there is no upper limit for other distilled liquors. You may serve alcohol if you are at least 21 years of age. City and county governments can set different sale hours. 18-, 19- and 20-year-old

	wine and beer production students can taste—but not consume—what they are making and studying.
Colorado	Spirituous, vinous & malt liquor is available in liquor stores and liquor-licensed drug stores only. Liquor stores closed on Christmas Day. Sunday sales restriction lifted on July 1, 2008. Liquor stores and liquor-licensed drug stores may have only one location, while beer may be sold in gas stations, supermarkets, and convenience stores. As of January 1, 2019, such establishments may sell full-strength beer. Appropriately licensed businesses may sell beer for both on and off-premises consumption. A small number of grocery stores are licensed as drug stores and sell full-strength beer, wine, and spirits. As an example, a chain grocery store that has pharmacy services at most or all locations may elect a single location in the chain as the licensed

	establishment to sell beer, wine, and spirits.
Connecticut	Sunday on-premises sales subject to local ordinances. Beer can be purchased at grocery/convenience stores. Spirits and wine can be purchased only at liquor stores. No off-premises alcohol sales on Thanksgiving, Christmas Day, and New Year's Day. Open container law applies only to drivers, not passengers.
Delaware	For off-premises consumption, alcohol may be purchased only in a liquor store, taproom, or a brewpub that has an off-premises license. Unless accompanied by a parent or guardian over 21, no person under 21 may enter a liquor store or taproom for any reason, even for the intent of purchasing only tobacco or lottery tickets. No sales of alcohol by liquor stores or taprooms are permitted during designated holidays including

	Thanksgiving, Easter or Christmas.
Florida	Sale, processing, or consumption of any liquor or spirit of greater than 153 proof is illegal. No retail sale of wine in containers larger than 1 gallon. FS 564.05 Supermarkets and other licensed business establishments may sell beer, low-alcohol liquors, and wine. Liquor must be sold in dedicated liquor stores which may be in a separate part of a grocery or a drug store. As of July 1, 2015, the restriction on 64-ounce refillable containers, or growlers, has been lifted and beer may be sold in quantities of 64 ounces, in addition to the previously legal 32 and 128-ounce sizes.
Georgia	Sunday off-premises sales from 12:30 p.m. to 11:30 p.m. allowed only by local referendum. In general, one may not be drunk in public. Though there is no state law prohibiting drinking in public, most municipal corporations

	and political subdivisions limit the possession of open containers of alcohol to private property, with notable exceptions being Savannah and Roswell. A charge of public drunkenness is only warranted when one is drunk in public, and his acts are either loud or disorderly.
Idaho	Alcoholic beverages exceeding 16% ABV can only be sold in Idaho State Liquor Dispensary stores, or contracted stores.
Indiana	Indiana prohibits the sales of cold beer by grocery stores or gas stations but allows cold beer to be sold from liquor stores. Minors, including babies, are not allowed to enter a liquor store. Indiana has a photo identification requirement for all off-premises transactions to anyone who is or reasonably appears to be less than forty (40) years of age. Public intoxication is a class B misdemeanor.

Iowa	If a controlled substance is detected in a person's system at or near the time they were operating a motor vehicle, they can be charged and potentially convicted of operating while intoxicated (OWI) even if they were not "impaired" by that substance.
Kansas	Kansas's alcohol laws are among the strictest in the United States. Kansas prohibited all alcohol from 1881 to 1948 and continued to prohibit on-premises sales of alcohol from 1949 to 1987. Sunday sales only have been allowed since 2005. Today, 29 counties still do not permit the on-premises sale of alcohol. 59 counties require a business to receive at least 30% of revenue from food sales to allow on-premises sale of alcohol. Only 17 counties allow general on-premises sales. Not all communities which allow off-premises sales allow sales on Sunday. Sales are prohibited on Christmas and Easter. Beer

	containing no more than 6.0% alcohol by volume may be sold in grocery and convenience stores. Before April 1, 2019, the only alcoholic beverage which grocery stores and gas stations were allowed to sell was beer with no more than 3.2% alcohol by weight. Other liquor sales only are allowed at state-licensed retail liquor stores. Kansas has comprehensive open container laws for public places and vehicles, public intoxication laws, and requirements for prospective on-premises or off-premises licensees.
Kentucky	A local ordinance may vote to permit Sunday sales at restaurants. Sales 2–4 a.m. only in Louisville. As of 2005 Sunday sales were allowed per state law, but may still be prohibited in some areas by local ordinance (as of early 2006, such a situation existed with smaller cities within Louisville Metro, though these cities have since changed local ordinances). Alcohol sale restriction and wet/dry (both by

| | drink and package) allowed by both county and city local option. Approximately 39 counties in the state (mostly eastern and southern counties) are dry, all alcohol sale and possession prohibited; 22 "moist" counties (with "wet" cities allowing package liquor sales in counties otherwise dry); 29 counties that are otherwise dry but have communities with local option that allow sales of liquor by the drink or under special exemptions allowing sales at wineries. Majority of wet counties are around major metropolitan areas (Louisville, Lexington, Covington, Bowling Green). Note: Beginning in 2013 Liquor by the drink and beer by the drink are available on Sundays in Louisville, KY beginning at 10:00 am. Bowling Green, KY recently began allowing Sunday sales in December 2013 for carry-out beer, wine, and liquor. Prohibition on liquor sales on Election Day was repealed effective June 24, 2013. Kentucky was one of only two states to still have Election |

	Day prohibition, the other being South Carolina.
Louisiana	Packaged alcoholic beverages of any strength may be sold in supermarkets, drug stores, gas stations, and convenience stores. Local municipalities may not restrict this. As a result, dedicated "liquor stores" are mostly specialty stores in larger cities, and some supermarkets have large selections of liquors and wines and compete based on liquor prices and selection. Alcohol can be consumed in the streets of New Orleans as long as it is in an "unbreakable container" (no glass) and may be taken from club to club if both establishments allow it. Otherwise, it depends on the locality. Most parishes other than Orleans Parish do not permit alcoholic beverages served on-premises to be carried out. However, many parishes and municipalities permit consumption of packaged beverages

	(for example, cans of beer) on the street. Glass bottles on the streets are prohibited. One can enter most bars at 18 years of age but must be 21 years old to purchase or consume alcohol. Also, it is legal in the state of Louisiana for a legal parent or guardian to purchase alcoholic beverages for their underaged child. Drive-thru frozen daiquiri stands are legal and common, but the police can arrest you for driving with an open container if you have put the straw in the cup.
Maine	ABV > Alcohol may not be purchased after 1 a.m. any day of the week, may not be purchased before 6 a.m. Bars and restaurants may serve until 1:15 a.m. On New Year's Day alcohol may be sold one hour later in all establishments. Wholesaling through state-licensed monopoly. Municipalities may prohibit the sale of alcohol by referendum; 56 towns have done so.

Maryland	Baltimore County prohibits sale on Sunday in some areas. In the counties of Montgomery, Somerset, Wicomico, and Worcester sale of alcoholic beverages is controlled directly by the county Liquor Control Boards, there are exceptions in Montgomery where some liquors are still sold in grocery store due to being grandfathered before the change of the law. Garrett County prohibits the sale on Sunday except in some areas. The sale of alcohol at grocery and convenience stores varies by county. There are no dry counties, but some individual voting districts within counties restrict or prohibit alcohol on a local-option basis.
Massachusetts	As of January 2016, no individual, partnership, or corporation may have more than seven off-premises licenses in the state, nor more than two in any city, nor more than one in any town. No individual, partnership, or corporation not resident or

| | headquartered in Massachusetts may apply for a license, although one may devolve thereupon. As of 2012-10-29, a Massachusetts driver's license, Massachusetts Liquor ID card, RMV-issued Massachusetts non-driver ID card, passport (issued by the US or a US-recognized foreign entity), US-issued Passport Card, and military identification card are the only acceptable proofs of age under state law. Out of state or Canadian driver's licenses/ ID's and other forms of identification do not grant the establishment legal protection if accepted as proof of age (and many establishments will not accept out of state licenses for this reason). On-premises regulations: No discounts at specific times (i.e. no "Happy Hour" discounts) or for specific individuals, no fixed-price open bar or all-you-can-drink (except at private functions), no more than two drinks per individual at any one time, no pitchers for fewer than two people, no drinking contests, no drinks as prizes, |

	no free drinks. Off-premises sale of alcohol is prohibited on the last Monday in May (Memorial Day), Thanksgiving Day, Christmas Day, and the day after Christmas if Christmas falls on a Sunday. Sale of alcohol is prohibited during polling hours on election days (subject to local exceptions). "Malt beverages" defined as having not more than 12% alcohol by weight.
Michigan	The Michigan Liquor Control Commission allows the sale of alcoholic beverages until 11:59 p.m. on December 24 and after 12:00 p.m. on December 25. On-premises sales are permitted on January 1 until 4:00 a.m. A local or county ordinance may restrict Sunday or Sunday morning sales. The state does not operate retail outlets; maintains a monopoly over wholesaling of distilled spirits only.State owns liquor until purchased and distributor acts as a delivery service for cases sold to retailers.

Minnesota	Local or County ordinance prevails for hours of operation for off-sale licenses. Growler sales allowed until 10 p.m. 7 days a week. Certain municipalities may establish municipal liquor stores; they are permitted, but not required, to exclude privately owned stores. Off-premises sales on Sundays became legal on July 1, 2017.
Mississippi	ABW > 5% wine and sparkling wine sold in state-contracted stores which are open from 10:00 am until 10:00 pm (Closed Sundays) statewide. Beer and light wine (ABW < 5%, ABV < ~6.3%) sold in convenience stores/supermarkets. Beer and light wine (ABW < 5%) may be consumed by persons age 18-20 with parental supervision. Governor Phil Bryant signed a bill permitting beer with 8% ABW/10% ABV on April 9, 2012. The bill went into effect on July 1, 2012. No sales on Christmas Day. No state open container laws. Complimentary

	alcohol all day and night in coastal casinos. In most counties, alcohol cannot be sold on Sundays. There are many dry counties in which it is illegal to possess alcoholic beverages, though some cities within dry counties have voted in beer sales.
Missouri	One of the most alcohol-permissive states, perhaps only behind Nevada and Louisiana: No open container law. No state public intoxication law. Liquor control law covers all beverages containing more than 0.5% alcohol, without further particularities based on percentage. Cities and counties are prohibited from banning off-premises alcohol sales. No dry jurisdictions. State preemption of local alcohol laws which do not follow state law. Certain bars in Kansas City and St. Louis grandfathered into the ability to double as liquor stores. Special licenses available for bars and nightclubs which allow selling alcohol until 3:00am in Kansas City, Jackson

County, North Kansas City, St. Louis, and St. Louis County. Grocery stores, drug stores, and even gas stations may sell liquor without limitation other than hours. Patrons allowed to take open containers out of bars in Kansas City's Power & Light District. Parents and guardians may furnish alcohol to their children. Missourians over 21 may manufacture up to 100 gallons of any liquor per year for personal use, without any further state limitation, state taxation, or state license. Obtaining a permit from the Federal Alcohol and Tobacco Tax and Trade Bureau and meeting other requirements under federal law probably still is required for private citizens to manufacture distilled alcohol - but not wine or beer - for personal use. Missouri law recognizes two types of alcoholic beverage: liquor, which is any beverage containing more than 0.5% alcohol except "non-intoxicating beer"; and "non-intoxicating beer," which is beer containing between 0.5% and 3.2%

	alcohol. Liquor laws apply to all liquor, and special laws apply to "non-intoxicating beer."
Montana	ABV > 16% wine sold in state-contracted stores, ABV < 16% may be sold in grocery stores. Some local ordinances restrict alcohol sales on Sundays. State-run liquor stores are closed on Sundays.
Nebraska	No on- or off-premises sales of spirits before noon on Sundays. All beer, wine, and champagne can be sold starting at 6 a.m.
Nevada	There are few restrictions on the sale and consumption of alcohol in Nevada except for age. The maximum abv of alcohol sold is 80%. State law also renders public intoxication legal, and explicitly prohibits any local or state law from making it a public offense. Alcohol purchase is only controlled in Panaca.

New Hampshire	Liquor sold in state-run stores, many found at highway rest areas. 14% ABV cap on beer. The state is the wholesaler of wine. State taxes beer $0.30/gal at the wholesale level.
New Jersey	Some dry communities in historically Methodist and Quaker communities in the southern part of the state. Though there is not a ban on selling alcoholic beverages at grocery stores, New Jersey limits each chain to two licenses, so with only a few exceptions, most supermarkets/convenience stores/gas stations/pharmacies do not sell alcoholic beverages. Also, liquor sales are only permitted in a separate department or attached sister store. The ability of a "liquor store" to sell other items, such as convenience store fare, is determined by municipality. Many towns permit beer/wine/liquor stores to sell non-alcohol items including convenience store items at the same register. In

	such towns, grocery stores including chains may theoretically apply for and receive a liquor license if the company does not already have two in the state. Bars are allowed to off-sale packaged goods. Except for Jersey City and Newark, all municipalities MUST allow off-sales of beer and wine at any time on-sales are permitted. However, since alcoholic beverages are generally only found in package stores, this right is rarely exercised. Alcoholic beverages by the drink as well as off-sales of beer and wine are permitted 24 hours a day in Atlantic City and Brigantine.
New Mexico	New Mexico issues two types of license for consumption on-premises: a full dispenser license allowing the sale of all types of alcohol, or a restaurant license permitting sale of beer and wine only. An additional Sunday permit is available which allows sale (on or off premises) on Sundays from 11am until midnight.

	Exceptions are the prohibition of alcohol sale on Christmas, regardless of the day it falls on, and a Sunday permit allowing of sale (on or off premises) until 2:00 a.m. January 1, if December 31 falls on a Sunday. Sunday permits are only available where approved by voters within a local option district. Selling, serving and giving alcohol to a minor is a class 4 felony punishable by up to 18 months in prison, except when "a parent, legal guardian or adult spouse of a minor serves alcoholic beverages to that minor on real property, other than licensed premises, under the control of the parent, legal guardian or adult spouse", or for religious purposes.
New York	Off-premises sale of wine and spirits is only at liquor stores, and beer is not sold at liquor stores; it must be sold at supermarkets and convenience stores. Exchanges for returned items are permitted (at store owners'

	discretion). Some counties may retain the Sunday morning beer prohibition which the state discontinued as of July 30, 2006. Twelve dry towns, mostly in the western region of state. Many counties have more restrictive off-premises hours, such as bans on beer sales overnight (hours vary). All liquor stores must be owned by a single owner, who owns that store and lives within a certain distance of it—effectively banning chain liquor stores from the state. New York City law does not allow open containers of alcohol in public. Distilled spirits may not be sold within 200 feet of a school, church, synagogue or other places of worship.
North Carolina	15% ABV cap on beer, 16% cap on unfortified wine, 24% cap on fortified wine. No "happy hour," "buy one get one free," or "ladies night" style specials allowed.

North Dakota	No off-sale on Thanksgiving Day. No Christmas Day on-sale, nor sales on Christmas Eve after 6 p.m.
Ohio	12% ABV cap on beer was removed on May 31, 2016. 21% ABV cap on wine. Some counties have more restrictive off-premises hours. The Division of Liquor Control does not operate retail outlets; it appoints private businesses to act as its agents and sell its products in exchange for a commission. Normal proof spirits (>21% ABV) are sold only in a limited number of agent stores. Many retail outlets sell diluted spirits (diluted by water to 21% ABV) under a more readily obtained permit. No intoxicating liquor shall be handled by any person under twenty-one years of age, except that a person eighteen years of age or older employed by a permit holder may handle or sell beer or intoxicating liquor in sealed containers in connection with wholesale or retail sales, and any

	person nineteen years of age or older employed by a permit holder may handle intoxicating liquor in open containers when acting in the capacity of a server in a hotel, restaurant, club, or night club. Beverages with less than 0.5% ABV can be sold/given to people under the age of eighteen if given by a physician in the regular line of his practice or given for established religious purposes, or the underage person is accompanied by a parent, spouse who is not an underage person, or legal guardian.
Oklahoma	As of October 1, 2018, strong beer (up to 8.99% ABV) and wine (up to 14.99% ABV) can be sold in grocery and convenience stores and can be sold refrigerated. Before this date, only 3.2% ABV beer could be sold in these outlets, and liquor stores could only sell strong beer and wine at room temperature. Distilled spirits are only available in package liquor stores. State law prohibits public intoxication,

	many counties and cities also prohibit public intoxication.
Oregon	Liquor, all of which is state-owned before sale to consumers, is sold in private liquor stores. These stores are approved by Oregon's Liquor Commissioners to act as sales agents on the state's behalf.
Pennsylvania	Spirits can only be sold at state-operated stores. All persons must be at least 21 years of age to enter a state-operated liquor store alone. Beer is not sold at state-operated liquor stores. Beer (but not wine) to go can be purchased at beverage outlets in any quantity. Before 2015 beverage centers could only sell 24 pack cases or greater. The rules were relaxed to permit sales of beer in any quantity in 2016. Beer and wine to go can be purchased in restaurants and grocery stores (at a separate point of purchase for alcohol and prepared foods sales in grocery stores) (six and

	12 packs/192oz max. purchase (two six-packs)) with Liquor Control Board–issued licenses. Sunday sales were prohibited in LCB stores until 2003 (selected locations) and beverage outlets (owner's option) until 2005. Special permits may be purchased for certain organizations for fundraisers once per calendar year, and are valid for a total of six days under the same rules governing restaurants. Grain alcohol prohibited as a beverage.
Rhode Island	All alcohol may be sold only in liquor stores. Bars may stay open until 2 a.m. in Providence only on Friday and Saturday nights and nights before a state-recognized holiday.
South Carolina	14% ABW (17.5% ABV) cap on beer Wine > 16% ABV sold in liquor stores No hard liquor sales after 7 p.m. and none on Sundays. No off-premises alcohol sales after midnight Saturday until 7 a.m. Monday, except in Aiken, Greenville, Pendleton, Spartanburg,

	Horry County, Colleton County, Richland County, Charleston County/city, Beaufort County, York County, and Newberry County.
South Dakota	14% ABV cap on beer
Tennessee	Wine may be sold in grocery stores. Liquor stores may remain open on Sundays, and liquor is permitted to be sold from retail stores for off-premises consumption. There are no liquor sales in OFF Premise Grocery Stores as of 8/2018. Retail package stores must be closed for business on Christmas, Thanksgiving Day, and Easter. Beer above 8% ABW /10.1% ABV must be sold in liquor stores. Open container law only applies to drivers, not passengers. It is legal to carry alcohol in a non-glass container on the Beale Street stretch in Memphis. While most clubs allow drinks to be carried outside, many do not allow drinks from outside.

Texas	No alcohol cap but ABV > 15.5% requires an additional license, so many places are beer/wine only. Wet/dry issues determined by city/county election. Liquor stores statewide closed all day Sunday. An alcoholic beverage served (on-premises) to a customer between 10 a.m. and noon on Sunday may only be provided during the service of food to the customer. Eleven Texas counties are completely dry. In many counties, public intoxication laws are vigorously upheld. Texas law permits consumption by minors (any age under 21) if in the "visible presence" of a parent, guardian or adult spouse. (Section 106.04) Possession by minors is permitted as part of employment or education, or in the visible presence of an adult parent, guardian or spouse, or supervision of a commissioned peace officer. (Section 106.05) There are also exemptions for minors requesting or receiving medical attention.

Utah	ABV > 4.0+% sold in state-controlled stores only. 3.2% ABW (4.0% ABV) beer may be sold at grocery stores and convenience stores. State-controlled stores close on Sundays and cease operations no later than 10 p.m. the rest of the week. Restaurants must buy from the state-controlled store (no delivery) at retail prices. No alcohol is served in restaurants without the purchase of food. Sales of kegs prohibited. Importation of alcohol into the state by private individuals generally prohibited.
Vermont	ABV > 16% beer and ABV > 16% wine is only available through state liquor stores (most of which are integrated within grocery and beverage stores). A 2008 bill allows the sale of beer in grocery and convenience stores up to ABV 16%
Virginia	Licensed supermarkets, convenience stores, and gas stations may sell beer

	and wine. Off-premises sales no later than 12 midnight. Liquor stores are owned and operated by the Commonwealth and are generally open 10am-9pm Monday-Saturday and from 12pm-6pm on Sunday.
Washington	Beer and wine are available in specialty stores, grocery stores, convenience stores, department stores, taverns, and other locations licensed by the Washington State Liquor and Cannabis Board. Spirits are available in stores greater than 10,000 sq ft (grocery stores, big-box liquor chains). There are two exceptions to the 10,000-sq-ft rule: 1) Former State and Contract Liquor Stores that reopened under private ownership may also sell spirits provided they have been issued a new license from the state. 2) Cities, mostly in rural areas, that do not have a store that meets the minimum floor space may be allowed to sell spirits if the Liquor Control Board

	deems that there are no sufficient establishments within the trade area.
West Virginia	12% ABV Cap on Beer. 75% of ABV spirits Permitted. Liquor, wine and beer products that are not already in closed packaging must be bagged before exiting retail locations. The state no longer operates retail stores (formerly State ABC Stores); Number of privately owned stores restricted according to county or city population. All stores are state-contracted; Bars and clubs must purchase liquor from state-contracted private stores in person. State retains monopoly over wholesaling of distilled spirits only.
Wisconsin	Wisconsin permits the consumption of alcohol by minors, provided they are being supervised by parents/guardians/spouses. Most municipalities have a uniform 9 p.m. restriction on all alcohol sales. Notable exceptions: Kenosha, Green Bay, La Crosse, Maple Bluff (near Madison),

	Baraboo (near the Dells). Supermarkets, liquor stores, and gas stations may sell liquor, wine, and beer. Law changed effective 12/7/2011 to allow all liquor sales to begin at 6 a.m. Nonalcoholic beer is not regulated by state law.
Wyoming	Clubs holding liquor licenses may be exempt from the hours of operation here specified by local ordinance or regulation of the appropriate licensing authority, but it does not seem to happen in practice

Printed in Great Britain
by Amazon